Once Upon a Schooner

Once Upon a Schooner

An Offshore Voyage in *Bluenose II*

Silver Donald Cameron

Formac Publishing Limited,
Halifax, Nova Scotia 1992

The MacAskill photographs in the first two pages of the photo section are reproduced courtesy of National Art Limited, the operators of Maritime Frame-It retail stores. Originals of these prints are available from them. Contemporary photographs are all by the author, except for the photo of *Bluenose II* in drydock, by Peter Brown, and the photo of the author, by Lulu Terrio. Back Cover photo: Ron Caplan. Front cover photo: courtesy Nova Scotia Department of Tourism and Culture.

Canadian Cataloguing in Publication Data

Cameron, Silver Donald, 1937-
  Once Upon a Schooner

Previously published as: Schooner.
ISBN 0-88780-225-7

1. Bluenose (Ship) 2. Bluenose II (Ship) I. Title. II. Title: Schooner.

VM395.B5C35 1992   387.2′2   C92-098684-6

Formac Publishing Company Limited
5502 Atlantic Street
Halifax, Nova Scotia
B3H 1G4

Printed and bound in Canada

52,605 X

Acknowledgements

The first edition of this book could not have been done without the cooperation of many people, not all of whose names appear in the text.

The Nova Scotia Department of Tourism was unfailingly helpful and gave me full access to their records and office facilities. The staff at the Killam Library of Dalhousie University, particularly Charles Armour, provided the papers of Angus Walters and the Bluenose Schooner Company and arranged for me to use their microfilm readers during hours when the machines are normally unavailable. Broadcaster Bill Fulton loaned me a whole box of taped interviews with South Shore dorymen, boatbuilders, and skippers — an unexpected treasure trove. Kerstin Mueller and the staff of the Eastern Counties Regional Library in Mulgrave, Nova Scotia, performed their usual miracles through interlibrary loan and demonstrated once again that it would be almost impossible to survive and work as a writer in rural Nova Scotia without their assistance.

Almost everyone I asked for interviews agreed to speak to me and most were very full and candid. Most of these debts are obvious in the book. I am particularly obliged to Peter Brown, Don Barr, and the crew of Bluenose II, from whom I learned a great deal and with whom I enjoyed myself immensely. For reasons which I hope are very clear in the text, I believe Nova Scotia is fortunate to be represented by people of such intelligence, good humour, and competence.

At the heart of everything is my tiny perfect wife, Lulu. It seems perverse to thank her for being what she is; but it seems right to thank the gods for bringing her into my life — and I do this every day.

Contents

Prologue

Once upon a schooner there was a peppery little skipper named Angus Walters. The schooner was *Bluenose*, and for twenty years Captain Walters fished her on the Grand Banks of Newfoundland for cod and raced her to glory at many a finish line, so that in the end, she became an enduring symbol of valour and victory in her own uncertain country, which urgently needed such symbols.

Twice upon a schooner there was a big affable skipper named Don Barr. The schooner was *Bluenose II*, and Captain Barr sailed her to the Great Lakes and the Eastern Seaboard, and to Panama, California, and the Pacific Northwest. She participated in world fairs and spread understanding of Nova Scotia among the unenlightened, and *Bluenose II* became the incarnation of the legacy of her fishing and racing ancestor.

Later upon the schooner was a writer named Silver Donald Cameron, who sought to understand the art and mystery of the schooners and their masters. To that end, he read old documents in quiet archives, viewed ancient films and photographs, and consulted old men with vivid young memories. Then, to cement his understanding, he slipped aboard *Bluenose II* in May of 1983 and sailed as an ordinary seaman in the second mate's watch while the schooner cruised from Lunenburg, where she had been built, to New Jersey, where she entered Atlantic City as the showpiece of a Parade of Sail.

The writer wrote a book about the schooners which briefly found favour with the readers of the country, but eventually sank without a trace.

Then, upon a cutter, the writer sailed around Cape Breton Island and wrote a book called *Wind, Whales and Whisky* which so pleased his readers that some called for another such book to read. Hearing this, the writer recalled his all-but-forgotten book about the schooners. Was it not another personal sea adventure with a cargo of history, humour, salty yarns and poignant episodes? Had it not been anointed by reviewers as "full of drama, love and laughter?"

The writer also realized that the country was soured with cultural dissension and political frustration, and needed to recall its symbols of valour and triumph. And he knew that *Bluenose II*, like other wooden ships, could not live forever. By now, indeed, *Bluenose II* was older than *Bluenose* had been when she sank off Haiti in 1946. But the writer learned that the ship's friends, public and private, were planning a campaign to build a new *Bluenose* schooner. A new edition of his book would salute the memory of *Bluenose*, the splendour of *Bluenose II* and the creation of *Bluenose III*.

There will be — there must be — a third *Bluenose* schooner, because a people seeking to define a great future must know the most noble achievements of their own past. Those who wish to excel will find their inspiration in men and women who sought the very limit of excellence with their finest ideas.

Once Upon A Schooner is the biography of such an idea.

Launching

Big Don Barr, 41, 6 feet 2 inches, and 225 pounds, buckets over the potholes of Montague Street in Lunenburg, Nova Scotia, in his tiny, tired Datsun B210, and opines that a man with a fifty-foot schooner today could make a dollar freighting. Barr knows about this. He has built boats, repaired them, sailed them, and loved them for two decades, and he once owned a fifty-foot schooner himself, a Newfoundlander which he lovingly restored and then sailed to the Caribbean.

"Look," says Barr, waving a hand towards the W. Lawrence Allen Dory Builders shop, "the problem those fellows are having is freight. The big market for their dories is down in Newfoundland, and it costs them a thousand dollars to ship a dory down there. Fellow with a big schooner could take half a dozen of them down, nested on the deck. Even if he only charged half-price, five hundred dollars each, he'd make three thousand dollars on the trip. And if you actually own a boat like that, living aboard is pretty cheap. You wouldn't have to do that more than two or three times a year to make a living."

Barr is captain of *Bluenose II*, the great replica of the greatest saltbanking schooner of all time. *Bluenose II* is owned by the government of Nova Scotia, so Barr is a civil servant. So is Peter Brown, who sits in the Datsun's back seat, and who did not like it when a writer described him as "a cheerful, round-faced, sandy-haired 35-year-old with the best job in the world," even though that is exactly what he is. Brown is operations manager for *Bluenose II*. He arranges the ship's appearances in Norfolk, New York, Philadelphia, Gloucester, Toronto, or wherever Nova Scotia needs promotion. He negotiates with shipyards and suppliers. He ensures that Barr has paint, marline, diesel fuel, and college boys, as required.

Barr and Brown are highly improbable civil servants. They do not particularly love the civil service, but they love their jobs, and their ship. Barr lives at Indian Point, a dozen miles away, in a gracefully renovated sea captain's home known as "Faulty Towers." Brown lives in the heart of Lunenburg in a Teutonic gingerbread Grimm Brothers fairytale house, and when the great schooner is laid up for the winter and Barr has decamped on his usual tropical vacation, Brown visits her every single day, checks the mooring lines, goes below and sniffs around, checks the water in the bilges, stands on the snowy deck, and is happy. For these few midwinter days, he does not have to share his beloved schooner with anybody — not even Barr, with whom he feels a powerful kinship. The ship is his, the saltiest thing in the saltiest town in Canada, and his alone. Brown takes a deep breath of the tarry, weedy, fishy waterfront air, grins, gets in his car, drives seventy miles to his desk in an office tower in the south end of Halifax, and smiles into the telephone all day.

Barr surrounds the steering wheel. He doesn't so much drive his Datsun as wear it, like a heavy jacket. He points at a tilting, antiquated, burgundy-coloured building on the right, with its fading sign: "A. Dauphinee and Son." The date is May 3, 1983, and this is the last day of business, ever, for that unique company, known locally as "the block shop." Arthur Dauphinee, not yet fifty years old, is closing up the family firm, going out of business — ending a world-famous Lunenburg establishment which made what landlubbers call pulleys and seamen call *blocks*. Not just any old blocks, either: regular works of art, turned and shaped out of mahogany, ash, or lignum vitae, according to the order, glowing and glistening in the sunlight with the deep rich grains of the wood under many coats of varnish. (Arthur doesn't easily admit it, but the varnish was not some arcane, secret formulation. He bought it by the gallon at Canadian Tire.) The block shop included a blacksmith shop, and its ancient workmen, using ancient belt-driven lathes and sanders and saws, made trawl tubs, oars, chain-plates, boathooks, dead-eyes, and many other ancient mysteries. But the main business was blocks — single blocks, doubles, triples; blocks with beckets and twisted shackles; blocks with ringbolts and screw eyes, turning blocks, cheek blocks, snatch blocks. Row upon row of them, hanging above the heavy, glue-lumpy work bench or lined up on the windowsill and gleaming in the sunlight. The blocks on *Bluenose II* come from Dauphinee's.

Arthur is giving up for many reasons. The building is sound, he says, but it needs repair. "I got a blacksmith working in a shed at the end of the building, and I'm worried for him every time it rains: he can't swim." He also cites the end of rail service to Lunenburg, the uncertainty of the post office, the difficulty of getting lignum vitae and good quality bronze. "Some of that bronze we're getting now, they say it's bronze but it's only brass. Hit it and it'll break off like a carrot." There's the red tape and paper-burden imposed on him by the federal government. There's the metric system. "They say we got to convert by the end of the year; it's compulsory. But these old machines aren't metric, and I got no customers that are metric, so they might as well just give me an order to close up, it comes to the same thing."

Above all there are the problems with freight. "The last order I sent to Hong Kong was a pain in the butt, and the last order I sent to Taiwan was worse. And you take a fellow down in Nassau that ordered a thousand dollars' worth of blocks from me: it cost him six hundred dollars to get the order shipped to him. Now how can a person do business in a situation like that? Years ago there always seemed to be a vessel somewhere going down to the West Indies, but there aren't anymore, so you got to send it by air, and it costs an arm and a leg."

Don Barr knows all this.

"A fellow with a fifty-foot schooner could carry any number of Dauphinee's blocks," he says as he drives. "Or you take Teddy Snyder over at Dayspring, now. Teddy sells boatbuilding lumber to Newfoundland, and the Newfoundlanders bring a big truck over here on the ferry, drive all the way down to Dayspring, load the truck, and take it back. It must cost them a fortune. With a schooner you could take a truckload of premium lumber down there for a lot less than that."

The return of commercial sail: the dream of every romantic on the world's waterfronts. It's coming, it's coming. Oil is finite, but the wind is forever.

Delbé Comeau, 34, a sinewy, bearded Acadian from Meteghan, occupies the fourth seat in the Datsun. Delbé was part of Don Barr's crew a dozen years ago, in the good ship *Hilda Gerard*, which Barr outfitted at Theriault's shipyard in Meteghan River. When Barr and his wife Tricia and their baby daughter finally weighed anchor, Delbé went with them. Barr sailed with fifteen dollars in his pocket. All down the coast of the United States, they would make a port, find the low-rent marina, and go to look for a job. They did the rigging on a square-rigger in Salem and built condominiums in Florida. All quite illegal, of course, but by the time the immigration and social-security sleuths got around to checking their papers, Barr and his merry men were long gone.

Years later, Delbé found himself back in Nova Scotia, working on *Bluenose II*. The ship needed a bosun. Delbé called Barr, who hustled up from Florida. When the skipper found he could splice wire, Barr became second mate. After the first mate committed such errors as upending a dinner table at a formal banquet in Florida, Barr became first mate. After another skipper accused the Nova Scotia cabinet of interfering with his management of the crew and using *Bluenose II* as the venue for wild parties, Barr became captain. His wife was not particularly pleased. She wanted to sail the world in *Hilda Gerard*. Now, while Barr is off in the ship promoting the province, Tricia offers bed-and-breakfast at Faulty Towers and hopes her husband will be fired. It seems unlikely.

We arrive at the Belroy Motel, two carloads of us. Wayne Walters sits at the next table. He is first mate of *Bluenose II*. A powerful, middle-sized man of thirty-five, Wayne is the grandson of Captain Angus Walters, who was part-owner, managing director, and skipper of the original *Bluenose*, the most fabled ship in our history, the ship that adorns postage stamps and the Canadian dime. Across the street is the house Angus Walters built before World War I. Wayne's uncle, B. J. "Spike" Walters, lives there now.

Over coffee, we swap stories and look out gloomily at the cold, raw, windy morning. Where will *Bluenose II* be a month from now? Nobody knows. Prince Charles and Princess Diana will visit Nova Scotia in mid-June, and the prince would like to see the schooner. The Department of Tourism is in anguish. The royals will only be in Lunenburg for an hour or so, not long enough to go sailing, and during May and June the ship normally makes goodwill tours of U.S. ports. Peter Brown has been arranging visits to Norfolk, Alexandria, and Atlantic City. The prince's whim has thrown his operations into royal confusion. It makes no sense to forgo thousands of dollars' worth of promotion just so that the royal couple can see *Bluenose II* in the distance. On the other hand, Nova Scotia is full of Loyalists and royalists, and most of them still dodder to the polls. The minister of tourism, who must settle this burning question of policy, is oddly enough, Lunenburg's own Member of the Legislative Assembly. If he draws the ire of the Hanoverian partisans, his name will not be Bruce Cochran anymore. Peter Brown's view is clear. A useful cruise should not be cancelled for ornamental reasons. But Peter is not the minister.

"I think that wind's gone down a little," says Brown, hopefully.

We had assembled at eight a.m. at the marine railway at the other end of town. Over our heads towered *Bluenose II*, high and dry on a railway carriage. She is, among other things, bloody big — 143 feet long, 27 feet at her maximum beam, over 15 feet from the railway carriage to the waterline, and another 6 feet above that to the rail cap. The top of her fore-topmast is 108 feet above her keel, and her mainmast rises nearly 126 feet. Her main boom is 81 feet 11 inches long, and the sail that will belly above it, at 4,100 square feet, is the biggest working sail in the world.

Her bowsprit thrusts seventeen and a half feet out beyond her stemhead, and a man can walk under her bilges the length of her keel without bending over. Peter Brown shows the twin propellers, the copper ground plate for lightning protection, and the intricate fitting of the wooden rudder port through which the rudder stock rises from underwater to the steering wheel on the afterdeck.

She cost a quarter of a million dollars to build in 1963, and 20 years later the province has spent another half million to rebuild her. Her planks are four-inch oak, and most of them are new. Her sawn timbers are massive eight-by-eight baulks of oak. The planks and their caulking required seven hundred pounds of oakum, one hundred pounds of cotton, and two to three tons of fastenings — nails, bolts, screws. The whole stern was rebuilt, the rail cap replaced, fittings removed, regalvanized, and refastened. The samson posts were replaced. Her lifeboats, which are fishing dories, were replaced at a cost of $1,150 each.

John Mosher, the Scotia Trawler executive in charge of the refit, broke the work down into areas of the hull and recorded the costs, section by section, on a computer. The next time he is asked to build or repair a Grand Banks fishing schooner he will be able to give very close estimates. This seems a fairly recondite skill, but Mosher says we may be surprised by what comes up.

The ship is absolutely breathtaking — her long, lean hull shining with fresh black paint, her yellow cove stripe and scrollwork bright and sharp, her bottom smooth and clean under its dull copper paint. Those long, flowing lines are what give the ship her speed perhaps. The keel is relatively short, only about fifty feet long, and from its forward end, her forefoot rises in a long, shallow curve right up to the waterline and beyond, with the suggestion of a hook right under the bowsprit. When the original *Bluenose* was built, Angus Walters wanted a little more room in the forecastle, where the crew lived, and raised her stemhead eighteen inches. This alteration gave *Bluenose* that unique, arrogant, upthrusting sheer line, with the bowsprit steeved well up, and it has been repeated in the replica. Down below, beside the keel, her planking rises almost straight and then curves sharply outward, rising abruptly to the waterline and recurving inward at the rail, a feature known as "tumble-

home." From amidships back, her long, sweeping underbody is almost straight. This is known as the "run," and a
straight clean run is one secret of a successful schooner. It
makes the water leave her smoothly, without creating ed-
dies and turbulence that will hold her back. The rudder is
tilted sharply aft, and the long counter stern, rising
smoothly from the waterline, terminates in an even more
sharply raked, heart-shaped transom.

Somewhere in here is the great secret, the reason nobody
could beat her — or one of the reasons, anyway, because
her captain was certainly another reason. They came
against her year after year, Canadian schooners and American, built to beat her, and some of them won a race or two,
but nobody ever recaptured the trophy she won in 1921, in
her first year of fishing and racing — the *Halifax Herald*
International Fishermen's Trophy, which said that she was
the fastest fishing schooner in the North Atlantic. The trophy
still stands in Spike Walters' front hall, holding dried flow-
ers.

But that was *Bluenose*, and this is *Bluenose II*, and we have
come here this morning to see her launched again — almost
a new ship, Peter Brown says, ready for another ten to
twenty years of service to the province that imagined her,
created her, cruises her, and is symbolized by her. But the
wind is still too strong.

"Once she's afloat," Don Barr explains, "you can't maneuver her until you get her going enough to have steerage
way, and with a wind like this she could blow all over the
place before you could get her under control. So we're
going to wait an hour or two and see if that wind dies
down. Let's go for lunch. Let's go to the House of Fish."

Peter Brown's background is marked by a love of boats
and a flair for management. He built small boats as a teen-
ager in Quebec, and has built others since. At the moment
he is restoring a fifty-year-old sailing dinghy. As a young
man, he took a job with the Coast Guard and made a trip
to the Arctic. Tiring of that, he enrolled in business administration at Laval University and became a salesman, later
a sales manager, for Goodyear Tires. Another Goodyear

salesman loaned him a summer cottage near Lunenburg, and Brown fell in love with the place.

"I was going to have to wait around for twenty or thirty years for the guy above me to retire, and I couldn't see the point in that," he said. "I figured I'd already reached the top in my field, and I wasn't thirty, and I wanted to live in Lunenburg. So I talked it over with my wife, quit my job, and we moved down here. We bought a house and settled in. No job, nothing.

"I went to work for Atlantic Bridge, here in Lunenburg. After a month or so, they made me sales manager of their Acadia gas engines division, and I lasted nine months before I got completely frustrated. The whole operation was so slow, the management was so unsystematic, they had no empirical basis for the decisions they were making, and so on.

"So I quit, and Shirley said, 'Well, what are you going to do now?' I said, 'I think I'll join you in the real-estate business,' which she had gotten into. She's a trained nurse, but she doesn't like to sit around doing nothing either, and she hadn't found a job nursing. I stayed in real estate three years — was president of the Board of Trade two years in succession, only the second person to do that. The other fellow became a senator, eventually. But real estate isn't a particularly good business in Lunenburg County because the prices are so low and you have to travel so far. You spend half a day driving away back in the woods to show a fellow a three-thousand-dollar lot.

"I knew Bruce Cochran, and by 1978 he'd become minister of tourism, and needed a temporary director of administration. So I went to work for him. The department was really a mess. Nobody knew who was reporting to whom, decisions weren't getting made, everyone was tangled in red tape. One good example is *Bluenose II*, which was essentially being administered by a committee. When Barr needed ten gallons of paint, he had to kick and scream to get one. So I recommended that the ship should really become a separate unit, with its own manager — and I said that was the job *I* wanted. Everyone was horrified. That was a step down for me. I didn't care. I hired my replacement, and trained him, and now I report to him." He throws back his head and laughs.

Back to the shipyard, bouncing along weatherbeaten old Montague Street, past the historic old firms, now dying off: Adams and Knickle, Atlantic Shipbuilding, A. Dauphinee and Son, Lunenburg Foundry and Engineering, Thomas Walters and Son. Vernon Walters, proprietor of that last one, is the only surviving marine blacksmith on the Atlantic coast, forging anchors, ringbolts, cranse irons, pintles, and gudgeons in the darkness of his smithy, doing his own galvanizing. He is a fiery little man who can if necessary provide all the hardware for a barkentine or a brig.

"You knew Vernon was hurt?" Peter asks.

"No! Vernon?"

"Yeah, someone brought him a bunch of oil drums to weld, and I guess one of them exploded. Bad burns, and a broken arm, and I don't know what else. He's still in hospital in Halifax."

Bad news, a good man in pain. And the silent question: Will Vernon be the next to quit?

Back to the shipyard once owned by Smith and Rhuland, who built one *Bluenose* in 1921 and another one forty-two years later, a company also defunct, bought out by Scotia Trawler. And the ship — the ship is already moving down the slipway, towards the water, gently lowered by inch-thick chain controlled by a belching old steam engine housed in a shack at the head of the marine railway.

Yelling and shouting, we bolt for the ladder that stands beside the ship on the railway carriage, scamper up onto the deck, and pause a moment. There was no great hurry after all. The ship is moving down into the water almost imperceptibly, a sharp contrast to the splash when she smoked down the ways right here, twenty years ago.

The impression you get, indeed, is not that she is sliding into the water, but that the water is rising about her. She is held upright by massive blocks of timber secured to one another with huge staples. At the sides of the carriage, a rickety catwalk connects heavy uprights, each with a winch and chain connected to the blocking. On each cat-walk, two men wait patiently for the water to take hold of the ship and lift her. A crowd has gathered around the head of the slipway, watching the ship return to her element. A photographer squints through his Nikon. Peter Brown stands in the ship's waist, a VHF walkie-talkie giving him access to John Mosher.

"Looks good," crackles the radio.

"Feels good," Peter answers.

The deck shifts. *Bluenose II* feels the ocean, starts heaving gently on her cradle. The men on the catwalks, in overalls, battered jackets, and slouch caps, start cranking the winches, moving from one upright to another, drawing out the wooden supports as the water reclaims the ship. Through the deck comes the vibration of one of two Caterpillar diesels. The engineer flicks his gaze back and forth between Barr and the gauges. Only one engine is running, but we only need one to get her to the wharf and anyway a little steel towboat is standing by — a rough, brutish little vessel, more like a battered jerrycan than a boat. "Dat little t'ing," grunts a workman, looking at her. "Christ, she vwas old vwhen I vwas a boy, you, and dat ain't yesterday."

The ship is afloat, and Barr orders the engine full astern. The schooner surges out into the harbour, checked momentarily by the lines from the starboard side of the carriage which hold her straight till she clears her cradle.

A hundred yards out, Barr orders the engine ahead. It is only a hop and a skip to the wharf, but Barr is not going there. He is a different man now: a tall, husky commander, standing proud on his quarterdeck beside Norman Whynot, the helmsman. And Whynot himself is no longer a polite, carefree young organizer for the Canadian Olympic Committee, which he was over the winter. He is part of the system now, a servant of the ship, an instrument in her master's hands.

"Hard aport," says Barr quietly.

"Hard aport, sir!" repeats Whynot, spinning the wheel. The great schooner swings to the left, away from the wharf, out into the harbour. Of all the ships and boats I have been aboard, this is the only one that seems bigger in the water than she does ashore. She is half the length of a football field, and she turns with ponderous grace, swinging the end of her bowsprit across the distant green of the golf course, past the anchored sloops and Cape Islanders, showing her elegant transom to the trawlers and work-boats of the waterfront.

"Steady there," says Barr.

"Steady, sir!" repeats Whynot, and *Bluenose II* heads for the harbour mouth.

"Which way is Bermuda?" Peter Brown asks his walkietalkie.

"Wha'?" comes the reply. "Bermuda?"

Barr takes his ship on a leisurely figure eight to Battery Point, at the mouth of the inner harbour. He has the engine put astern, and he smiles with Brown to feel the smoothness of the maneuver. Before the refit, reversing the engines would shake the whole afterdeck. Then he brings her back to the wharf, slowly, with dignity, judging his distances and the inertia of his vessel. Men scramble ashore with lines. The engine shuts down. It is not a perfect docking, but the ship is not in shape yet, either, with her deck a tangle of disconnected rigging, paint cans, discarded bits of rail cap. There will be another three weeks of hard work before the recommissioning ceremony which seems warranted by the expenditure of $500,000. After that, she will be ready to sail — if, in fact, she is going anywhere.

With the ship secure, I duck below for my gear. When I come back on deck, *Bluenose II's* people have vanished, and the ship is given over to the workmen again. I scan the wharf and the waterfront, peering under the bilges of the yachts standing in their cradles on the shore and then I see them: Brown, Delbé Comeau, bosun Rick Moore, Don and Tricia Barr and their daughter Cheryl. Six faces, looking back at this ship of dream and legend. Six faces, all smiling.

Departure

At ten a.m. on May 24 the mood in the lounge of *Bluenose II* is restless. It's a bone-chilling, blustery morning, with bursts of rain pattering on the peaked skylight overhead. The royal couple are to be disappointed. *Bluenose II* was expected to sail south at eight o'clock. But the electronic marvel that navigates from artificial satellites couldn't be installed until this morning, and, late last night, Delbé Comeau squirmed through the bilges and located a small but worrisome leak in the hull. John Mosher and another diver dropped into the frigid water at seven this morning, plugged the leak with a pine wedge and some oakum, and nailed a lead tingle over it. The bilges were pumped dry at ten minutes after nine, and if there is no more water in them by noon, the ship will leave. Diesel fuel will be delivered at eleven. The engineer is up at the shop having a piece of the bilge pump repaired.

The lounge is full of people who are not making the voyage to Atlantic City, Alexandria, Norfolk, New Haven, Newport, and Boston. Tricia Barr, with neighbours from Indian Point. Wayne Walters' wife Nancy. Mary Gupthill, Delbé's lady.

What do you say, after you've said good-bye?

On deck, young crewmen in yellow oilskins are lashing down the dories, packing endless numbers of life preservers into deck boxes, stowing coils of rope. Others are up in the town, doing their last-minute business — buying sea boots, going to the bank, mailing letters. Mentally, the crew has departed. They hang in some kind of awkward limbo, their bodies ashore, their imaginations out at sea. What will they be wearing out there? a new hand asks the first mate.

"Probably your breakfast," answers Wayne Walters.

I wander around Lunenburg this miserable morning. A dozen men are gathered in the Atlantic Shipbuilding store, chatting and telling stories. A handful of women are shopping in Oxner's IGA, or at the Scotia Trawler Foodmaster.

Two bored clerks in Kinley's Drugstore resent the intrusion of customers.

Ah, Lunenburg.

Physically, this is one of the loveliest of Maritime towns. Its crenellated, filigreed houses, painted teal, citron, and terra-cotta, march up the steep hill from the waterfront in orderly ranks. Its baronial old school glowers down from the hilltop. Its waterfront is crowded with wharves and sheds and shops. Its extensive museum offers movies, an aquarium, and three complete ships — the rumrunner *Reo II*, the trawler *Cape North*, and the schooner *Theresa E. Connor*. Lunenburg fairly reeks of tradition and craftsmanship, of sound values and tested principles.

It is also, by the very same token, parsimonious and intolerant, suspicious of innovation and of outsiders alike, obdurate, narrow-minded and rude. Lunenburg County, in general, detests its shiretown. The town, in turn, views the rural areas with lofty disdain. "How many fishing captains came from the town of Lunenburg?" demands a county man. "I'll tell you — not one. They came from Blue Rocks, Feltzen South, Back Centre — all around the county. But not a single one from the town of Lunenburg." But Lawrence Tanner, custodian of the *Theresa E. Connor*, smiles at Norman Whynot, who comes from Mahone Bay, six miles away, and says, "You're just six miles short of bein' a good feller."

Lunenburg has no public debt at all. The town pays as it goes. Admirable. As a result, it has an incomplete water and sewer system, despite the highest property taxes in Nova Scotia, while no municipality in Nova Scotia receives less in grants from the provincial government. Not so admirable. The fifty-five-man volunteer fire department, of which Brown is a member, has raised about $250,000 in three years to buy three trucks and a paging system and to upgrade the fire hall. The town of Lunenburg has contributed about $10,000 — and legally it owns all the equipment.

Lunenburg has always been capable, cranky, unique. After the Treaty of Aix-la-Chapelle in 1748, Britain moved to consolidate its hold on mainland Nova Scotia. The area had been British in theory since 1713, but almost all its people were French. The British founded and fortified Halifax in 1749 and encouraged "foreign Protestants" from the king's German principalities to immigrate. Industrious German peasants settled Lunenburg in 1753, and the town still has a German flavour to its architecture, its speech, and its notions. Women sweep the sidewalks in front of their houses. Common law marriages are not approved. The county eats and exports sauerkraut, and until recently it firmly believed in witchcraft. Names like Hiltz, Pentz, Wentzler, Zinck, Zwicker, and Eisenhauer dominate the phone book.

The other big name is Bluenose — Bluenose Inn, Bluenose Taxi, Bluenose Golf Course, Bluenose Lanes, Bluenose Electronics. Touching, this reverence for the finest of their splendid schooners, but when Angus Walters tried to save her from her ultimate destiny as a cut-down Caribbean freighter, the prudent burghers kept their plump purses zippered. A wealthy citizen named R.C.S. Kaulback offered to match all donations from the townspeople and opened a bank account into which contributions, however small, could be made anonymously. After several months, he closed the account. Nobody had deposited anything. At the time, Lunenburg's per capita income was surpassed in all of Canada only by that of Westmount, Quebec.

Ah, Lunenburg.

By twelve-thirty the tension aboard *Bluenose II* is palpable. The satellite navigator is in place, the pumps are working, the tanks are full, the bilges empty.

"Let's go, let's go!" hisses Wayne Walters.

The ship's company assembles on deck. Kisses and handshakes. The visitors climb the gangway. The engines start. The sails are freed. The lines are cast off, and the ship backs away from the wharf, the lane of water between the two evoking a much wider gap.

There is something particularly poignant about a ship's departure, a faint aroma of death and high adventure. The engines go full ahead. David Stevens steers a wide semicircle towards the harbour mouth. The people on the dock, growing smaller by the minute, are going back to their houses and offices — safe places, by and large, which will not sink or overturn or be swallowed up. The eighteen men on the schooner feel relief and anticipation, and a small cold touch of fear. A ship, even this one, is a small work of man to pit against the immensity of the oceans. Over a thousand Lunenburgers have died at sea, and whole ships have simply vanished — sailing away like this and disappearing forever over the misty horizon.

And so the schooner sets out with her young, ardent crew, plunging and bucking into the teeth of a stiff southeasterly that heaps up the water and drives it peaked and frothy into Lunenburg Bay. Her diesels drum, sheets of spray are flung out from her bows, her long bowsprit dips below the horizon and corkscrews up into the charcoal sky. She makes seven and a half knots over the ground. Her crew is bundled up in long underwear, heavy pants, sweaters, oilskins, toques, and mittens. The wind is biting, the cold strikes into the bones.

An hour later she is just south of Cross Island, which sits plumb in the mouth of Lunenburg Bay, and her green crew, chewing cloves and Gravol, are setting sail. The vessel heaves and twists, tossing her head, rolling from side to side, while the mates give their orders: Take a turn on the windlass with the main peak halyard, cast off the sail stops on the jumbo, sheet the foresail home. The crew has made sail only twice before, on trial cruises yesterday and last Saturday, and eight of them are completely new to sailing.

"They're slow yet," says Don Barr, watching all the activity from his post by the wheel, "but by the end of the summer they'll be able to get all her sails set in fifteen minutes. We're only hoisting the four lowers today. This would be heavy weather for a small yacht, but it's just a nice sailing breeze for us."

Her canvas arching aloft, *Bluenose II* falls off on a course parallel with the distant, cloudy coastline, doing nine knots. The motion is more comfortable, as it always is under sail, but *Bluenose II* is "lively," as Don Barr puts it.

Most sailboats pitch slowly and regularly, rolling a little when reaching across the wind. *Bluenose II* is never regular. She hunts and noses and worms her way through the waves, that huge main boom dipping towards the water and rising again, her stern lifting high above one trough and sinking abruptly into the next. I have spent a lot of time in boats and have never been seasick, but I am feeling — augh — uneasy, and some of the crew are distinctly ill.

"I've never been sick in anything else," Delbé Comeau remarks sympathetically, "but I've been sick twice in this vessel."

Even seasoned officers decide to skip supper tonight. I am making this trip in place of Norman Whynot, who has other business to attend to. I am therefore in Delbé's watch from twelve to four, midnight and noon. I should get some sleep — but when I try, I find myself sliding fitfully in and out of wakefulness, clinging to a mattress, nauseated and bedevilled by the ceaseless groaning and squawking and chirping of the ship's fabric as she twists in the confused seas. I go on deck late in the evening, gulping for fresh air. The ship has altered course, steering 220 degrees to pass east of George's Bank en route to Atlantic City, and she is heeling from 15 to 20 degrees, swinging back 5 degrees to windward at times. Ian Morrison, a curly-headed apprentice businessman from Kentville, suggests I try his berth, which is on the lee side of the ship. Chocked up against the inner skin of the hull, I nap gratefully for an hour.

Seasickness is often stimulated by nervousness, but I am not particularly nervous. I trust this ship. She struck a hurricane not far from here on her maiden voyage in 1964, and won the praise of everyone aboard for her handling of it.

"It had been a bad fall with one storm after another," remembers Ellsworth Coggins, then her skipper. "I talked to the weatherman before we left and he said there was a storm coming up from Virginia, but from all reports it would veer to the north and we'd have three days to get clear of it. If we were well out to sea, we'd only catch the edge of it. So we went.

"Well, instead of veering north, it turned south and east, right where we were. We ran before it, hard, as long as we could. The winds were up around eighty knots. I decided to heave to, and we double-reefed the foresail. That took us twenty-eight minutes, and while we were doing it the wind just stopped. We were right in the eye of the storm.

"Then the wind came back from the exact opposite direction. I remember Angus Walters standing in the forward companionway, with his barometer in his hand. He was eighty-two then, and he'd brought his own barometer, he wouldn't trust ours. He was saying, '*The glass is still falling, skipper, the glass is still falling.*' It was a very low glass, that's true. I've never seen one lower.

"We were hove to for three days. The whole storm lasted five days. It was nice to have everything new, you know, but it was still untried — that was the worrying thing about it. After the wind went down to about fifty, the seas got up to about forty feet. That's the way it goes. When it's blowing really hard, the wind blows the tops right off the seas.

"The sea doesn't get up until the wind drops down some. That's the dangerous time, but we made out all right. The time I lost a man over, heading south in January 1969, it was right after a gale when the seas were high. We had taken in the mainsail on a dirty night, and we just put a couple of stops around it to hold it till daylight. The next morning it was still blowing a good breeze, the wind coming one direction and the sea another, and while the men were furling the main, I saw a rogue sea coming down on us right on the beam.

"I called out to hold on — and it broke right over us, twenty to thirty feet high. It cleaned the deck. The life rafts were gone, the compass was gone, the skylights were stove in, the engine room was flooded, and when the decks cleared I saw one of the men climbing back over the rail, and two more in the water."

Bluenose II was hove to, but even with "her head under her wing," she made a bit of headway. The crew got life rings to the men in the water, but they had to work the two men around to the lee rail before hoisting them aboard. The ship was moving, and the stern was rising and falling so heavily that they were worried the men's heads would be smashed if they got under it. The first man — Craig Harding, now a lawyer in Liverpool, Nova Scotia — was alert, talking to the crew, and helping them maneuver. The second man, Neil Robitaille of Yarmouth, appeared dazed and didn't respond. By the time they got Harding aboard, Robitaille had lost his grip on the life ring and was gone. Despite an extended search by the Coast Guard, no trace of him was ever found.

"You torture yourself for months afterwards," Coggins says. "You keep asking yourself, did I do everything that could be done? Is there anything I could have done different? One thing that made it bad was the steering — that same sea had bent the worm gear so it took three men to turn the wheel. That gear is made of solid three-and-a-half-inch metal bar, so it gives you some idea how hard that sea hit." Clearing the bilges with pumps dropped by a Coast Guard plane, escorted by a Coast Guard vessel, *Bluenose II* limped to Bermuda. It took two weeks to repair the damage.

After the 1964 hurricane, Angus Walters said the original *Bluenose* had known only one gale as bad. In September 1935, *Bluenose* was returning from England having taken part in the celebrations for the Silver Jubilee of King George V. The Lunenburg schooner had occupied the king's own mooring, and the king himself had entertained Walters aboard the royal yacht *Victoria and Albert*. "We chewed the rag for a while," Angus reported. "He was a very nice, ordinary sort of fella."

Six days out of Falmouth, after many hours of squally winds, heavy seas, and rain, *Bluenose* lay hove to under storm trysail and jumbo. At one-thirty in the afternoon, the wind hauled to the west-southwest "with hurricane force," noted Walters in his log.

Vessel laboring very hard and terrific seas running. Laying now under bare spars. Impossible to do anything. Continued pouring oil through toilets and by oil bags. At 10 p.m. a terrible sea hit vessel heaving her almost on beam ends, breaking for'gaff and for'boom, smashing boats, deckhouse engine box, throwing cook stove over on side. Tons of water going below doing other damage and causing vessel to leak very bad. Had to keep continuing pumping. Vessel opening up aft by pounding heavy. At 3 a.m. kept off and ran her under reef jumbo.

There followed a desperate struggle as the passengers and crew, pumping constantly, shifted pig-iron ballast, and Walters wondered whether he was going to have to cut away the vessel's masts to keep her afloat. There is a story that during the long moments when the vessel lay on her side, with her masts flat to the water, Walters shouted, "*Get up, you black bitch, get up!*" Slowly, with a long shudder, she did. Among the passengers was Commander Ian Black, a destroyer captain of seventeen years' experience, who said, when they made Plymouth twenty-four hours later, that it had been "the most terrifying sea I have ever encountered," and who considered that he owed his life to the seamanship of the Lunenburgers and the qualities of *Bluenose*.

It was not the only time *Bluenose* and her skipper cheated the sea. In April 1926 the schooner was lying at anchor inside the curving northwest bar of Sable Island, the almost mythic graveyard of shipping 150 miles off the Nova Scotia coast, when a southwest gale sprang up. *Bluenose* was instantly in danger, dependent on her anchor alone to keep her out of the breakers. Walters prudently prepared his storm sails, and waited. At about six o'clock that evening, with the wind at seventy knots and the seas from thirty-five to forty-five feet high, a great comber smashed part of her bulwarks away and snapped her anchor cable.

Anyone who has seen a bottle in the surf will understand the threat. A ship going ashore on Sable blows sideways towards the beach until her keel trips on the bottom in the trough of a wave. Then she rolls over and over, smashing herself to pieces and battering everyone aboard to death. It has happened to five hundred ships. It must be a particularly horrible way to die.

Walters immediately made sail and began trying to beat to windward out of the trap, counting on *Bluenose's* weatherliness and power to drive her out to sea in the very muzzle of the gale. He sent the crew below and lashed himself to the wheel for six hours, praying that the tortured rope and canvas would hold, sailing almost parallel to the shore, gaining a few feet of sea room on each tack.

"I never expected to see Lunenburg again," he said later. "I stayed to the wheel because I didn't trust anyone else. They might have been as good as I was, but I knew the vessel. But I never knew through all that night when we were going to scrape bottom. You couldn't see the seas coming. Just see the white capping up. Half the time you didn't see the white, it was snowing so hard. You could hear 'em coming. Get your feet planted, not that it would do any good. You'd get a grip but the sea would knock it out. It was wet, I can tell you. Sometimes I was all under, just come up to get my breath.

"When the wind hauled after midnight, I was about all in, to be honest with you. Worst gale I've ever seen on the Banks. But she kept heading up, biting her way into the gale. Don't know as any other vessel could have done it."

When they cleaned her up the next day, they found sand on her decks: a souvenir left by the angel of death.

No, I am not worried about this dancing, creaking ship. But I am undeniably seasick. If I weren't so miserably nauseated, I would be annoyed. Me, seasick! Did I not skipper my own little schooner around the Maritimes with never a tremor in my belly? Did I not keep my dinner inside me during an appalling Irish Sea crossing when most of the other two hundred fourth-class passengers were depositing their beer and bangers on the saloon floor?

Perhaps this nervous, exploratory motion is related to the ship's speed. *Bluenose* was a working fisherman, certainly. But she was built to race as well, and it was her racing, not her fishing, that made her one of her country's proudest legends.

The impulse to race seems to be as much a part of sailing as the curve of the canvas itself, or the tremble of the helm in one's hand. The tea clippers raced from China to Europe. The Bahama fishing smacks race every year at the regatta in George Town. Nova Scotia sealers used to race home from the Bering Sea, all the way down the Pacific to Cape Horn and all the way back up the Atlantic. Some of this racing is based solidly and squalidly in considerations of commerce. The first oysterman home gets the best price, the first fruit schooner from the Azores is likely to bring London the freshest, least bruised produce. But the racing impulse is independent of economics. "Sailing ships have always raced," writes Allan Villiers, who sailed in the grain ships that once raced from Australia to England via the Horn. "While two survive, they always will." Wendell P. Bradley, who wrote with deep insight about the last fleets of working sail, found the working sailors' love of racing to be their most pronounced common feature, because it evoked "their passion for sailing, their possessiveness about their vessels, and their absorption in the details of their calling."

In this sense, the great fishing schooners of Atlantic Canada and New England had always raced — raced to the fishing grounds, raced home, raced to the Magdalen Islands for bait. They also raced formally in local contests long before the International races of the 1920s and 1930s. In *Roving Fisherman*, F. W. Wallace describes a couple of stirring encounters between Capt. John Apt's *Albert J. Lutz* and Capt. Harry Ross's *Dorothy M. Smart* before Digby audiences which included such luminaries as the Duke of Connaught, then governor-general.

By the same token, the fishermen followed the America's Cup races with professional interest and patriotic partisanship. Canadians, taking the British view, considered that the cup itself had originally been won by Yankee guile rather than seamanship. The schooner *America*, built in New York specifically to race in England, captured the 100-Guinea Cup off the Isle of Wight in 1851 because, Canadians thought, her shallower draught allowed her to cut closer into the shoals, shaving a full nine miles off the race course. The Americans were asked to pause for ninety days to allow a British challenger to be built. Instead, they hurried home and offered the cup as an International Trophy under rules made and administered by the New York Yacht Club.

These rules have been the source of much bad feeling ever since, and until 1983 the cup was never won by a challenger. In 1920 the challenger was *Shamrock IV*, owned by the tea tycoon, Sir Thomas Lipton. (It is said that Sir Thomas endeared himself to Americans and increased the sales of his products by losing graciously year after year. More recently, Baron Bich cannot have harmed the sales of Bic lighters, pens, and razors by mounting a similarly futile series of French challenges.) The defender was *Resolute*, notably tender, at her best in light winds. *Shamrock IV* won the first two races, Resolute the next two. The deciding race was called off by the New York Yacht Club because of dangerously high winds — of twenty-three knots. This ruling favoured *Resolute*, which eventually won the last race in lighter airs.

One can imagine the reaction among fishing captains accustomed to driving their schooners through snowstorms and gales in the open Atlantic. Angus Walters heard about it when he reached Lunenburg after his summer trip to the Banks, with the hold of his schooner *Gilbert B. Walters* packed with salted cod. He was not impressed.

Neither was Senator W. H. Dennis, publisher of the Halifax daily newspaper, the *Herald*. That same week, Dennis met a group of business friends for lunch — Reg Corbett, H. R. Silver, Harry de Wolf. They considered the whole history of the America's Cup, and the slipperiness of the decision to cancel the race, and their derision was monumental. Legend has it that a cook aboard a Lunenburg schooner discharging fish at Halifax muttered about setting up a real race, for fishing schooners, and the idea surfaced at the lunch table.

By the time the Haligonians called for the check, they had formed themselves into a committee to oversee what became known as "the *Halifax Herald* North Atlantic Fishermen's International Competition." They raised four thousand dollars in prize money, and Dennis's newspaper contributed a four-foot-high silver loving cup as a trophy. They wrote a careful Deed of Gift and enlisted the premier of Nova Scotia, the mayor of Halifax, and a young aspiring naval architect named William Roue among the trustees. And they sent the word to Gloucester, Massachusetts: Choose your best schooner and send her to Halifax.

Competing schooners had to be working fishermen, with at least one season on the Banks behind them. They could be no more than 145 feet overall, 112 feet on the waterline, and they must carry all their ballast inside. They were to race with their regular fishing complement of sails.

Angus Walters followed all this with interest. *Gilbert B. Walters* was a moneymaker — she had paid for herself twice over in a single season — and she was fast. When the Halifax committee made it known that they would bear the cost of preparing the Canadian schooners for competition, Angus Walters entered. On October 11,1920, just two months after the America's Cup fiasco, *Gilbert B. Walters* led the fleet across the starting line and held the lead right into the home stretch, closely pursued by Capt. Thomas Himmelman, in *Delawana*.

"Then it happened," Walters later recalled. "A guff of breeze carried away the fore-topmast. Tom Himmelman made the best of that one and soon we were dropping astern. The *Delawana* crossed the finish line about five minutes ahead of us."

A week later, the Gloucester schooner *Esperanto* danced into Halifax under the command of Capt. Marty Welch, a native of Digby. Although she was fourteen years old, *Esperanto* was a dainty little vessel, 107 feet in length, built for quick trips from the grounds with fresh fish for Boston as well as for longer voyages to the Banks. *Delawana*, like most Nova Scotian schooners, was a husky, burdensome vessel, designed for long trips to the Banks in summer and cargo voyages to the Caribbean in winter. Since the speed of a sailing hull is largely a function of her length at the waterline, *Delawana* had a natural advantage — but she lost the first race by a full eighteen minutes. The crew worked feverishly overnight, shifting and removing ballast stones and hoping for a lighter wind the next day. Angus Walters, meanwhile, had noted that *Esperanto's* ballast was iron, which concentrated her weight low down and made her better able to stand up to her sail. He reckoned Himmelman would lose, "although he was every bit as good a sailing man as Marty Welch."

Walters was right. In the second race, *Delawana* led *Esperanto* throughout, only to see Welch make a bold dash through the shoals along the shore of Devil's Island. The Gloucesterman was owned by Gorton-Pew Fisheries, and R. Russell Smith, one of her owners, was aboard. When Welch grew concerned about the danger of sailing so hard in such shallow water, Smith cried, "To hell with the kelp and rocks, Marty, keep her to it!" Welch did, and the trophy went to Gloucester.

Esperanto carried a new broom, symbol of victory, at her masthead when she entered Gloucester harbour on November 7. No vessel before or since has ever had such a welcome. The next few days were a whirl of banquets and receptions, cheering crowds, and gloating sailors. In Halifax, meanwhile, the men who had started the races were determined that their trophy should be brought home. They found Bill Roue at his office on Upper Water Street where he worked in the family firm manufacturing ginger ale. But Roue had been an enthusiastic amateur naval architect since childhood, spending many hours building and sailing model yachts, noting the effect of different amounts of ballast, different hull shapes, different rigs, different configurations of keel and rudder. His first commission, an open cockpit cutter named *Babette*, was designed for F. H. Bell of Halifax, and was still sailing satisfactorily at the age of forty. Bell knew B. B. Crowninshield, the noted Boston naval architect, and once had occasion to show him *Babette's* lines.

"Who drew these up?" asked Crowninshield, after studying the drawings.

"Oh, just an amateur," Bell answered.

"Well, he won't be an amateur long," replied Crown-inshield.

Roue had designed several other yachts, but he was still at the bottling plant when Dennis and his colleagues approached him. The very idea of engaging an architect was a radical departure from tradition. Normally, a fishing schooner was designed by her builders, who carved a model of one side of the ship from a block of soft pine, shaving it away until it looked right, and then building the vessel to conform to the "side model." But the Halifax men wanted something special: a schooner that could pay her way as a working saltbanker and still beat the best that Gloucester could send against her.

"Sure," said Roue, "I'll try my hand at a schooner."

He worked through the fall of 1920 on the design — an immense schooner, fully 120 feet on the waterline. He paid particular attention to the matter of ballast, agreeing with Angus Walters that a low centre of gravity was the key to a vessel's sail-carrying power. He took the plans to the committee three weeks before the deadline — and the committee rejected them. The ship was too big. Could Roue scale her down?

He could not. A vessel's shape is a complex interplay of shapes and forces, and the proportions which work at 150 feet of length are altogether wrong at, say, 100 feet. One simple example: a skiff on the beach may be half as wide as she is long. Imagine a schooner with similar proportions. She would look more like a swimming pool than a sailing vessel.

So Roue went, literally, back to his drawing board. He still had the basic work he had done over the weeks just past, and he had the plans of *Zetes*, a highly successful racing sloop built to his design a decade earlier. He returned to the committee in three weeks with his new design — the design that was to make him famous. Several of her features disturbed her builders. The rudder, for instance, was streamlined, thick at the forward edge and fading away towards the trailing edge. Smith and Rhuland were accustomed to the exact opposite. The vessel tapered dramatically at the stern, too, ending with a very narrow afterdeck, just wide enough for the wheel and the main-sheet. This also offended her builders and distressed her skipper as well. But, said C. H. J. Snider of the *Toronto Telegram*, who sailed twelve races aboard her,

> when the helmsman was in water up to his knees on the lee side of other fishermen's wheels, in *Bluenose* he was working dry-shod.... When *Mahaska* or *Henry Ford* or *Columbia* or any other racing fisherman would get a knockdown, the water would rise twelve feet up the deck to leeward and pour aft in a raging torrent, com-pletely filling the gangway between the lee side of the cabin house and the lee rail, and swirling up to the wheel box. *Bluenose* would be going along just scuppering it, her lee rail out, and the tumblehome and tuck-in of her long, tapering quarters keeping ev-erything dry aft.

Howard Chapelle calls her "a powerful vessel well able to carry sail in the hands of her captain, who was an ag-gressive, unsportsmanlike, and abusive man, but a prime sailor." Roue called her "Design #17." Smith and Rhuland called her "Hull #121." Some of her owners wanted to call her *Cavendish*, in honour of the governor-general, the Duke of Devonshire. But the name chosen was the old, sardonic nickname for Nova Scotians themselves: *Bluenose*. In De-cember the governor-general made a special trip to Lunen-burg to drive a golden spike into the new vessel's keel. The town was hung with bunting, and the harbour was crowded with vessels. The duke arrived early and was hustled off to a convivial private gathering from which he emerged distinctly wobbly. He was given a silver mallet with which to drive the golden spike. He swung — and missed. He swung again, and missed again. Someone took pity on him and drove the spike for him. The duke said the experience was unique in his lifetime.

Angus Walters didn't think much of the name *Bluenose*, but he thought a great deal of the schooner; that winter, indeed, he thought of little else. The Halifax committee had asked him to be her skipper. Walters never really knew why. At first, he refused. He had a good ship, only three years old. He was making good money with her. What if the new vessel failed as a racer? The Halifax men would have little further interest in her, and he would have parted from a good ship and been left, perhaps, with a poor one. But his brother John urged him to accept, offering to skipper *Gilbert B. Walters* himself. Angus then agreed, but stipulated that the ship would be capitalized at $35,000 — a high price, $10,000 more than the usual cost of a schooner — of which Walters would control $20,000 worth. The Haligonians would be partners in his ship, not he in theirs. With these points settled, John Walters took the old ship south that winter, while Angus stayed in Lunenburg to badger and hound the shipwrights. He nearly drove them foolish.

The new schooner was launched March 26, 1921. A special excursion train came from Halifax. The waterfront was jammed, and people were perched all over the nearby buildings and the steep little hills. Motion-picture cameras whirred. At ten minutes to ten, when high tide was due, the workmen began knocking the blocks and shores away from the vessel. At ten o'clock she began to move, and Audrey Smith — daughter of her builder, niece of her captain — smashed a champagne bottle against her hull and christened her *Bluenose*. The schooner shot down the ways and coasted fifty yards out into the harbour. The tug *Mascot* towed her to Zwicker's Wharf, where the speeches were made and where the ship was to be rigged.

Sometime that day, Richard Smith was asked what he thought of the ship.

"I don't think nothin' of her," he answered. "She's different from any vessel we ever built. We built her as close to the Roue lines as we knew how. If she's a success, he gets the praise. If she's a failure, he gets the blame."

Wednesday — Graveyard Watch

At midnight, I'm wakened by the change of watches. The officers have cabins astern, near the wheel, but I am berthed in the hold with seven other ordinary seamen. Four more sleep in the forecastle, up in the bow of the ship, where the motion must be furious. I struggle into my sea boots and sailing suit — orange insulated overalls, made by Mustang, the envy of the crew on this miserably cold voyage — and come on deck to find *Bluenose II* sliding along through a glossy, heaving sea under a silver canopy of overcast, backlit somewhere by an invisible moon. It's surprising how well one can see around the decks. Delbé Comeau reports that the engines are off and the schooner is doing eleven knots under sail alone. It doesn't feel like it, although she is certainly slipping along.

"It's deceptive," remarks Don Barr. "People always underestimate her speed. We've come close to having some bad accidents that way. Small boats don't realize how fast she's coming, and don't get out of the way until it's almost too late."

Something similar happens to small boats in the lee of those vast, ghostly sails. *Bluenose II* carries 12,200 square feet of sail, and behind that wall of canvas there is no wind. Small boats sail towards her — rail-down and working hard — and are suddenly jerked upright when they enter the schooner's wind shadow. Then *Bluenose II* passes, and they are abruptly blown flat in the water again. Wayne Walters likes to tell about a Sunfish skimming down towards *Bluenose II*, her sailor hiked far out on a trapeze to keep her upright. She sailed behind the mainsail and instantly capsized, firing the fellow headfirst in a backward dive into the water.

Is *Bluenose II* as fast as her ancestor? The question has been debated all up and down the coast for the last twenty years. Those who sailed with Angus Walters say no, almost universally. *Bluenose* was clocked at 14.15 knots, and Doug Pyke, now a retired fishing executive, who was aboard, has

established that the U.S. Coast Guard ship *Harriet Lane* was
doing 16 knots when *Bluenose* passed her in a 1938 race off
Gloucester. Another crewman in the same race remembers
the speedometer touching 18 knots at times as she surfed
down waves.

But Don Barr, Peter Brown, and others who know the
new ship well believe *Bluenose II* is faster. She carries somewhat more sail and its synthetic fabric is smoother and
holds its shape far better than the canvas sails of fifty years
ago. On a majestic charge down the Florida coast in 1978,
Bluenose II made a timed run even faster than her ancestor's
best: a sustained average of sixteen knots.

Now, somewhere south of Cape Sable, Delbé Comeau
looks up at that enormous mainsail apprehensively. It is so
heavy and it puts such a strain on the rig that it cannot be
allowed to slat. In light winds and a lumpy sea, it must be
taken in. Conversely, it cannot be taken in when the wind
is really strong. Flogging as it came down, the sail could do
serious damage to the ship or her crew. It can only be
carried in winds between about fifteen and thirty knots.
Without it, the ship will not go to windward. Even in a
gale, though, it would not be likely to blow out. That fif-
teen-ounce Dacron is so strong that it bent the steel bars of
the weaving machine when it was being made. If *Bluenose
II* were caught in storm conditions with her mainsail up,
she might be dismasted or knocked down before that sail
would rip. If the sail area could be reduced by reefing, she
could carry it in almost any imaginable wind; if need be,
her crew could risk lowering it in a gale. Hood Sails, in
Toronto, who built that mainsail, said they could not give
it reef points, even though they were in the specifications.
I would not have accepted the sail without them, myself.

That mainsail is responsible for the astonishing run in
Florida. *Bluenose II* left Jacksonville heading north with a
forecast of moderate winds. Before the crew had grasped
what was happening, the wind had piped up to fifty knots,
and they had all four lowers set. For the next five hours, all
the way to Savannah, her officers watched the rig and the
anemometer, and prayed.

"We were hard on the wind, and the wind was right off the land, so there was no sea at all," says Delbé Comeau. "The masts were bending like fishing rods, and when she lay down in a gust, the water was away above the lee rail. It was magnificent, all right, and it was scary, too. Those lanyards at the ends of the shrouds hold the masts in the ship. They were old lanyards, and there was no stretch left in them. But when we got to Savannah and set them up again, we got a good two feet of slack out of each of them.

"And when we checked the times on the chart, we found she had averaged just about exactly sixteen knots for the whole five hours."

These night watches are a good time for stories, for meditation, for long, searching conversations. The ship's company sleeps. Only the watch on deck remains wakeful. Each of the four crewmen takes two half-hour turns at the wheel, while the mate watches for ships, plots the ship's progress every hour on the chart, makes notations in the log, decides whether courses or sails should be changed. There are long silences, as the ship noses her way over the unquiet water: men standing grouped around the wheel, staring out over the sea, gazing up at the rigging, balancing against the motion. Lost in thought, companionable but relieved of any need for speech, thinking — what? We would be hard pressed to say.

I am thinking of my stomach, which is more rebellious than ever. Delbé looks at my pallor and offers to excuse me from the remainder of the watch. I shake my head. I am stubborn and I do not want to fail to do my share. Besides, I would probably feel worse in the confines of my berth.

"We're likely going to have to get that mainsail in," says Delbé. "That wind's still dropping off."

My watchmates are all young Nova Scotians. David Stevens, a student at Acadia University, is the son of an old friend of mine, the descendant of generations of shipwrights, sailmakers, seamen. His great-grandfather was sail trimmer on the original *Bluenose*. His father, Murray, rebuilt the interior of the ship in 1980, using afrormosia, mahogany, stainless steel, and teak. Even the floor of the engine room is mahogany plywood. David's great-uncle, Harold Stevens, made most of the sails for *Bluenose II.*

Charlie Randle is just setting up a business selling home computers, but he has taken this chance to sail aboard *Bluenose II* because it is the kind of adventure a business career might never permit again. Brian Steeves looks like a beach boy, or perhaps a fullback, but he is actually a student of philosophy at St. Mary's University, and he wants to cycle across America on his ten-speed bicycle.

They are curious about *Bluenose* — her record, her fate, her master. Is it true, they wonder, that she was never beaten?

No, I reply, she was beaten, but never when her championship was at stake.

Bluenose could have been lost before she had a chance to win. She left for the Banks in April 1921, and on the way out she fell into company with *Gilbert B. Walters.* As always, such a meeting was an occasion for a "hook," or race, and the new schooner strode easily away from the old one. Angus Walters, who loved both vessels, must have seen it with mixed feelings. To the end of his life, he believed that the *Walters*, properly rigged and trimmed, "would have given the *Bluenose* a damn hard time."

The Grand Banks of Newfoundland can be a dangerous place; they are directly on the routes from Montreal and New York to Europe, and frequently swaddled in fog generated by the mixing of the cold Labrador Current with the warm Gulf Stream. That first summer, Angus Walters was called on deck one night to confront a full-rigged ship looming out of the fog, under way, and ready to cut *Bluenose* in half. Nobody aboard the ship responded to the schooner's bells and horns, and finally Walters took two crewmen and rowed over to the stranger in a dory.

> I sung out and somebody on deck answered me. I asked what he intended to do, run us down? Could he not see our riding lights and the vessel right there?

He said that his ship could not keep off. I said, "If she will not keep off, why do you not back your yards and let her drift away from us?"

Certain his vessel would be demolished, Walters stayed near her in the dory. But some trick of tide and current carried the big ship clear, and *Bluenose* lived.

She made a good fishing season — one of her catches was the largest ever landed by a saltbanker in Lunenburg — and in September she was hauled out to be scrubbed and painted for racing.

First, *Bluenose* had the Canadian championship to win. The elimination races began October 15, and no fewer than five of the competitors boasted names in which a vowel was thrice repeated, for good luck — *Delawana*, *Alcala*, *Independence*, *Donald J. Cook*, and *Canadia*, along with the prosaic *J. Duffy* and *Ada R. Corkum*. *Canadia* had been built by Joseph McGill in Shelburne, and like *Bluenose*, she was as much racer as fisherman. In the first race, *Bluenose* crossed the starting line first and turned the first corner four minutes ahead of *Canadia* and nine minutes ahead of *Alcala*. The schooners tore into a fog bank as the wind freshened, and the three leaders emerged at the halfway mark within three minutes of one another.

But now, for the first time, *Bluenose* began to show her special wizardry — a devastating ability to work to windward, tacking back and forth into the breeze, making up ground into the teeth of the wind; and the harder it blew, the closer she pointed and the faster she footed. She slashed across the finish line a full four minutes ahead of *Canadia* and seven minutes before *Alcala*.

Her windward ability brings smiles even yet to the faces of men who knew her. Doug Pyke sits in a basement den festooned with side models, blocks, photographs, and memorabilia, and says, "There were others that could reach and run with *Bluenose*. There were even some that could beat her, on a run. But to windward? No way."

The second race of 1921 was *Bluenose* weather, with a raw and gusty twenty-five-knot wind. *Delawana* stayed with her on the downwind legs, and actually nosed ahead of her at the halfway mark, but when the two turned to windward, *Bluenose* shot away again, crossing the finish line a cool sixteen minutes ahead of *Delawana.* "That was her real strong point," says Spike Walters. "She could fetch in one tack what others would take two tacks to reach." Angus, in fact, came to count on that quality. On several occasions he was inattentive or careless on the downwind legs, falling behind needlessly. He knew he could always make up to windward what he lost off the wind.

It is customary to praise her beauty, and certainly *Bluenose* was beautiful, particularly in still photographs. Some elderly film footage of her races survives, however, and seeing her in motion is something else altogether. She bores into the frame from the right, coming so fast that the viewer involuntarily gasps. She is not pitching or rolling. She is slicing through calm water, and she looks like an avenging angel — aggressive, irresistible, relentless. Beautiful? Yes, but with the implacable, streamlined beauty of a shark or a bullet. The projection room is dead quiet, and the schooner crosses the screen in about four seconds, moving as steadily and remorselessly as a machine tool or a fast freight, and then she is gone.

"Jesus! "

"She's doing over fourteen knots right there," says the quiet voice of Peter Brown. He smiles. Everyone reacts to that shot in the same way. Nobody can believe that anything goes that fast under sail.

In New England, back in 1921, a nasty situation was brewing. A Boston syndicate headed by Fred L. Pigeon of the Pigeon Hollow Spar Company had hired the famous yacht designer, Starling Burgess, to design a vessel that would beat both Gloucester's defender and Nova Scotia's challenger. The result was the narrow, deep, and fast schooner *Mayflower*, which at once provoked a storm of protest in Gloucester. *Mayflower* was not, said the Gloucestermen, a fishing schooner at all, but a racing yacht in fishermen's oilskins, designed for speed, not for fishing, and certainly not for salt fishing on the Banks, as the rules required. Gloucester would boycott the races. Angus Walters said he would, too.

There is a fine line between the workboat and the yacht. Indeed, many celebrated yachts began their lives as workboats: the Bristol Channel pilot cutters sailed by H. W. Tilman; the oyster smack *Spray*, rebuilt by Joshua Slocum for the world's first solo circumnavigation; the little Lunenburg schooner *Cimba*; the Norwegian rescue boats designed by Colin Archer, to name only a few. On which side of that fine line did *Mayflower* fall? H. R. Silver, one of *Bluenose*'s most ardent backers, went to Boston, examined *Mayflower*, and saw no legitimate reason to disqualify her. Edgar Kelly, editor of the *Halifax Herald*, took precisely the opposite view:

> When the *Herald* started this thing, the idea was to foster the development of real honest to goodness fishing schooners. If the *Mayflower* owners succeed, it will develop into-another America's Cup proposition, and so end, as abruptly as it began, an endeavour to promote a growing industry. I have never had any illusions about *Mayflower*. She is an out-and-out schooner yacht. Indeed, the term "schooner yacht" appears on her sail plan. The action of the slick Yankee yacht fanciers is Not Cricket.

Alas, H. R. Silver had already announced that the decision about *Mayflower's* eligibility was up to the American Race Committee. The controversial schooner had indeed made the required fishing voyages — yacht or no, she ultimately fished for eighteen years — and the American committee accepted her. None of the Gloucester schooners appeared to race against her. Then the International trustees met and declared *Mayflower* ineligible. (Someone had also noticed that she was a foot too long on the waterline, a useful technicality.) The *Mayflower* group sent a representative to plead their case, but to no effect.

With the Boston schooner out of the way, Gloucester fielded five contenders. *Esperanto* had struck the submerged wreck of the *S.S. State of Virginia* off Sable Island in June, and had gone down in twenty minutes. Her crew was picked up by the Gloucester schooner *Elsie*, and it was *Elsie*, captained by Marty Welch, that was victorious and was escorted by a U.S. destroyer to Halifax. She was a noble and lovely vessel, built in 1910, and for years a high-liner in the Gloucester fleet. Like most Gloucestermen, she was small — 106 feet long, 25 feet in the beam, with a draft of 11 feet 6 inches. After her joust with *Bluenose*, she was used as a trial horse for *Gertrude L. Thebaud*, the last Gloucester vessel to tackle the Canadian champion and she ended her days in Newfoundland, where she sank in 1935.

Angus Walters had made a quick trip to Lunenburg for some final tuning up, and on the way back he fell into company with none other than *Mayflower*, on her way to Halifax for the races. It was the only time the two ever sailed together, and an informal "brush" ensued. *Bluenose* drew steadily ahead, but Walters could see that *Mayflower* was not really being pushed. On the other hand, reaching was not *Bluenose's* best point of sailing, either. Walters dismissed the brush as "just another way of makin' us feel good," and did not consider it a serious race. He would have loved to race *Mayflower* properly, though he did not consider her a fishing schooner. He was confident he could have beaten her. He had looked her over carefully in Boston, he said long afterwards, and had concluded that "if that goddamn thing can beat the *Bluenose*, I don't know nothin' about a vessel."

A nice example of the international bitchiness that ultimately disfigured these races is highlighted by the New England author James B. Connolly, who writes that the *Mayflower* "so decisively outsailed every vessel she hooked up with during her first summer on the Grand Banks that the Canadian Committee barred her from the International Contest. To revenge herself on the *Bluenose*, the *Mayflower* went over the race course that first year, and her manner of outsailing the *Bluenose* was scandalous to view." But it was Gloucester that first objected to *Mayflower*, and *Mayflower's* cruise along the racecourse, in company with *Delawana*, was made under four lowers only and with a shipload of spectators. Nobody but Connolly seems to have noticed that she outsailed *Bluenose*.

But everyone noticed that *Bluenose* outsailed *Elsie*. Halifax Harbour was full of spectator boats, and the schooners were accompanied by the Canadian government ship *Lady Laurier*, among many others. From the *Laurier*, a full account of the races was broadcast by wireless — the first such use of radio in a marine event. Outside the offices of the *Halifax Herald*, two model schooners were suspended on wires. The same device was placed across a street in downtown Lunenburg, and as the reports came in from the races, the two schooners were moved along their wires to show who was winning, and by how much.

Elsie sailed well against *Bluenose* in the first race on October 22, leading off the mark and holding the lead until Walters forced Welch to luff up in smooth water just outside the harbour mouth. *Bluenose* then bore away, and reached the first mark a minute and a half ahead. The next two legs were off the wind, and the two vessels were only twenty-seven seconds apart at the third mark. Then came a twelve-mile beat to windward in what were by now strong winds. Within a tack, *Elsie* found herself half a mile astern. Her fore-topmast broke off, depriving her of the balloon jib and fore-topsail — but she could not have carried them much longer in the wind then blowing. Nevertheless, Angus Walters doused the same sails in *Bluenose*. It made no difference. *Bluenose* romped home thirteen minutes ahead.

Watching all this from the deck of the press boat, Capt. Alden Geele, one of *Elsie's* owners, jumped up and down on the deck, crying out, "Poor little *Elsie*! My poor little *Elsie*!" Over the forty-mile course, *Bluenose* had averaged eleven knots. That evening, one of the Lunenburg sailors told Marty Welch's wife that *Elsie* would certainly have won if it hadn't been for something in the water that afternoon.

"What was that?" inquired Mrs. Welch innocently.

"The *Bluenose*!" laughed the Lunenburger.

Two days later, Marty Welch again got the better start, and again the two vessels were locked together through the downwind legs. But *Bluenose* took over commandingly in the long windward leg, and was three miles ahead at the finish, winning the series.

It is easy to imagine the jubilation in Halifax that night, as fishermen, skippers, and ordinary Nova Scotians pounded one another on the back and treated one another to drinks. A big wooden crate came aboard *Bluenose* containing a dozen bottles of champagne — a generous compliment from *Elsie's* owners. The gesture was appreciated by the somewhat nonplussed fishermen, but the wine was not. "To hell vwit' dis apple chuice!" someone cried. "Break out de rum!"

And that, by all accounts, is what they did.

Aboard *Bluenose II*, the wind is unmistakably slackening. The ship rolls heavily, spilling the wind from her sails, then filling them again. The three-thousand-pound main boom swings ominously from side to side. Delbé Comeau looks aloft anxiously, then goes below. Don Barr emerges with him, and they consult in low tones. That mainsail will have to come down. All hands on deck.

The men emerge, yawning and stretching. Floodlights on the spreaders create a harsh chiaroscuro, black, white, shiny, on the pitching, wet deck. The thousand-pound gaff lunges heavily from side to side as the sail swings down, folding itself into its lazy jacks. The skipper himself hauls on the mainsheet, takes the wheel, handles the quartertackles. Men hurry through darkness from one urgency to another, muzzling that enormous sail. Rich Moore leaps up off the quarterdeck, trying to hook quarter-tackles through a metal bale on that lethal boom. Only a low stern bulwark stands between him and the sea, and if he were to go over now we would be lucky to get him aboard before he died of hypothermia. The same thought flickers through his mind and makes him careful.

The crew lines up along the main boom, on top of the deckhouse, the engine hatch, the wheel box, heaving the stiff fabric into some semblance of a furl. I am hanging over the bulwarks, unable to help, not having been through the sail drills at the wharf and feeling baggy with nausea.

It is over, and the men filter below to strip off their oilskins and try again to sleep. For five of them, the next watch is just two hours away. And I am hanging between the shrouds, my face pointed towards the disorderly waters, retching and spewing orange acid chyme on the clean black topsides of the schooner.

"You don't have to stay," says Delbé a few moments later. "Probably you should go below."

Backed against the deckhouse, swaying with the ship, I have been asleep on my feet, drifting between distorted, surrealist dreams and a reality which seems itself like a distorted dream of darkness, fog, and motion. I'm no use to anyone, anyway. What am I trying to prove? That I am as good a man as these kids? That I understand the seaman's perspective — that the ship comes first and personal discomforts second?

There is a strange, winged creature flying through the blackness, iridescent purple under its wings …

"Go below," says Delbé's voice. And I go.

With their five thousand dollars in prize money in hand, *Bluenose*'s owners sent their ship on two trips to Puerto Rico during the winter and paid a 15 percent dividend to the shareholders of the Bluenose Schooner Company, Limited, on their first year of operation. Over her lifetime, the schooner would return 151 percent on the dollar, most of it during the spacious days of the 1920s.

The company itself was downright miserly. All that winter Bill Roue struggled to collect his fee. The usual fee is 5 percent of a vessel's cost, but Roue agreed to accept 3 percent and had a hard time collecting anything. He made nine trips to Lunenburg during the building, running up expenses of $152.20. H. R. Silver wrote to Walters in October to say that he had advanced Roue $168 out of his own pocket, that he thought the bill should be paid, and that he did not like "to approach him with any proposal of compromise." After letters and sight drafts had failed, Roue put the matter in the hands of his lawyers, who in late February were still writing to the company. Though the details are unclear, the matter was eventually settled. Unhappy though Roue must have been about his dealings with the Bluenose Schooner Company, the success of *Bluenose* enabled him to stop making ginger ale and commence a long and satisfying career in naval architecture. He designed tugboats, ferries, and pilot boats as well as yachts. During World War II he invented a specialized sectional barge; $29 million worth of these barges were eventually built. His later designs also included a three-masted schooner based on *Bluenose* to be used as a training ship by the fledgling Canadian navy, and another racing schooner, *Haligonian*, designed to beat *Bluenose*. In 1980 the star attraction at the Halifax Boat Show was a sleek blue sloop with long, sweeping overhangs, a swan among the blocky factory-built boats beside her. She looked a little like *Bluenose*, of which she was indeed a descendant. She was a Roue 20, produced in fiberglass — a bit of ancient poetry reborn in the newest of marine technology.

Roue was not the only one to bump his nose on the stinginess of the Bluenose Schooner Company that winter. On its income-tax return, the company listed its five thousand dollars in prize money as a gift, and thus tax-exempt. Nonsense, said the Dominion tax commissioner in Halifax. The Lunenburgers did not argue. Instead, in classic Maritime fashion, they put the screws on their member of Parliament, who put the screws on the taxman. The company got its exemption. Similarly, in 1924 the company appealed against its property-tax assessment by the town of Lunenburg. Its schooner was assessed a trifle higher than other newer schooners. Never mind that its schooner happened to be the greatest of them all.

While the Bluenose Schooner Company was minding its money, rivals were building ships. Two new challengers appeared in the Canadian eliminations in 1922, *Mahaska* and *Margaret K. Smith*, along with the familiar *Canadia*. Paddy Mack, *Mahaska*'s skipper, had boasted all summer that his ship was faster than the champion on all points of sailing. When she was beaten by twenty minutes in a thirty-mile race, Mack was so furious that he tore off his trademark, a derby hat, and danced upon it on the deck.

Bluenose was escorted to Gloucester by the destroyer HMCS *Patriot*. The American challenger was the big new *Henry Ford*, like *Elsie* a product of Boston's Capt. Tom McManus, the acknowledged master of fishing-schooner design, and built in the famous Essex yard of Arthur D. Story. She was bigger than usual — 138 feet long, 26 feet in the beam — and she had been dogged by bad luck. On her way down the Essex River after launching, she had snapped her towline, drifted ashore, and stuck fast. Left alone overnight, she floated herself and drifted aground again, this time on Wingaersheek Beach. There she stayed for four days, while tugs hauled valiantly at each high tide. She may have been strained by the ordeal; she was said to have sailed better on one tack than the other.

If the *Ford's* luck was bad, her leading rival's was far worse. *Puritan* was designed by Starling Burgess, built at the J. F. James and Son Yard in Essex, and launched March 15, 1922. She was awesomely fast and lovely. On her maiden voyage on April 17, she easily ran away from a subchaser doing eleven knots. Shortly thereafter she fell in with *Mayflower* and left her astern, too. Her skipper, Capt. Jeff Thomas, said she was readily able to reel off fifteen knots.

He made two trips with *Puritan*, and on the third she killed herself. On June 23, when Thomas believed himself to be twenty miles short of Sable Island, he sailed right over the northwest bar of that vicious sandbank, ripping out her keel and jamming her rudder up through her stern. All her crew were rescued — but *Puritan* vanished forever, a victim of her own speed.

So *Henry Ford* became the challenger under Capt. Clayton Morrissey, the son of a skipper, the brother of another, and the nephew of three more. Morrissey's first command had been his father's ship, the *Effie M. Morrissey*, which he took over at nineteen when his father fell ill. This gallant little vessel, built for Morrissey's father and named for his sister, had perhaps the most remarkable life of all the saltbankers. Built in 1893, she fished out of Gloucester for a dozen years, then out of Digby, Nova Scotia, for nine more years before she was sold to the Bartlett family of Brigus, Newfoundland.

In 1925 the *Morrissey* fell into the hands of Capt. Bob Bartlett, the explorer. During the next two decades, Bartlett took her on more than twenty voyages to the high Arctic and established her as one of the noblest ships of this century. After Bartlett's death, she was sold for a freighter, and for the next thirty years she carried cargo between New England and the Cape Verde Islands. In 1976 she was acquired for Mystic Seaport, in Connecticut, where she remains to this day. She was a working vessel for eighty-two years, which must be a record of some kind, and she is over ninety now. She is probably the only original sailing saltbanker left afloat anywhere.

Thirty years after his initiation as a skipper, Clayton Morrissey in *Henry Ford* jockeyed for the starting line only a few yards from Angus Walters and the big black *Bluenose*. The wind was light, and the race committee decided to postpone the start for half an hour. Neither skipper ever admitted having seen the signal. Both were under heavy pressure from their supporters, and eager to get going.

"What about it, Clayt?" called Angus.

"Okay by me," answered Morrissey.

The race was on, committee or no. The judges fired a gun to draw attention to their signal. When that failed, they sent Patriot flying after the two schooners. The destroyer failed too, and the ships kept battling furiously to gain the advantage in the light breeze. Both finished after the six-hour time limit, but *Ford* had led *Bluenose* all the way and crossed the finish line ahead.

"Chalk one up for Clayt," said Angus. "We'll take him tomorrow."

But the committee was mightily ruffled and declared the race unofficial. Both Morrissey and Walters objected. The race had been sailed properly, *Ford* had won, the skippers were satisfied. But the committee was immovable.

Ford's crew was furious and equally stubborn. They were not going to be jigged about by brass hats on committee boats. They had worked hard all day. They were not about to be told it hadn't counted. They were going to carouse, and the hell with racing.

But among the dignitaries in Gloucester just then was Josephus Daniels, former U.S. Secretary of the Navy, and he met with the crew. "Never let it be said," he is supposed to have cried, "that the men of the Pubnicos and Clarke's Harbour were the ones to trail Old Glory in the dust."

Pubnicos? Clarke's Harbour? Well, yes: Morrissey himself was from East Pubnico, and most of his crewmen were from southeastern Nova Scotia. After this strange appeal to their patriotism, they went out and sailed again the next day. And the results were the same: light airs, a race that amounted to a drifting match, and a two-minute victory for *Henry Ford*. The committee wanted to declare this race unofficial, too. Evidently the vessels had crossed the starting line slightly before the gun. Again Walters and Morrissey objected, and this time they prevailed. It is worth noting that if the first race had counted, Ford would have won the cup.

The vessels took a day off — and, according to Walters, that day off was fatal for Clayton Morrissey. *Bluenose* went out for a tune-up run, flying her four lowers. Soon after, Henry Ford appeared.

"Clayt comes out with his big blow-bag crew, their tops'ls flying," Walters later recalled. "It was squally. First thing they find, they're layin' in the water. That took the life out of Clayt and scared the life out of his crew." It was always Walters' opinion that the Americans generally over-canvassed their boats and that their vessels were tender. "That night," he grinned, "we prayed for wind."

They got it, and next day Morrissey's wife came over to ask for a postponement. Walters refused. "I didn't come here to stay till Christmas-time," he said. "I'm going out to the line, and if you're there, fine."

Bluenose set out and *Ford* soon followed. The wind was about twenty knots, and "the *Ford*, she went adrift," said Walters. "Before the wind she was all right. Anyone can go before the wind. But the last leg was to windward. She fell over and damn near stayed there. Thank God it was the last leg, or they would have called it off.

"Around the last turn, we were no farther apart than from here to the corner. At the finish, they were so far to looard you could hardly see them."

Like *Elsie* the year before, *Ford* carried away her topmast in that race, which led some of her shoreside partisans to claim that the weather wasn't fit to race in. Once again, Angus Walters struck the sails his rival could no longer carry, but he himself hadn't even worn oilskins, he said, and he hadn't been wet. Yes, it had been blowing, but the water was smooth. It was not weather to lose a topmast in.

Back at the wharf, *Mayflower*'s people were trying to set up a race with *Bluenose*. Walters was agreeable, but he wanted to wait until after the official series. His confidence in his ship was never better expressed than in a remark during one of these races with *Ford*. The two vessels had been sailing close together, and the crews had been swapping insults. When they reached the windward mark, Walters called out, "If you gentlemen got anything more to say to us, say it now. From now on, it'll cost you postage."

The series ended with another breezy race, and another victory for *Bluenose*. But tempers were high (there is a story that a group of shrewd and disloyal New Englanders had wagered $75,000 on *Bluenose*, which may account for some of the sullen anger in the air), and when Walters' nephew and crewman Boodle Demone asked for money to go ashore and celebrate, Walters refused.

"They were sorer than hell over in Gloucester," Walters later explained. "I said no because I knew what it was like. That night, he and one other feller went anyhow. They were the only ones from the vessel that did."

The next morning, Boodle Demone's body was found under a wharf. He had drowned. By accident, they said.

"It has always been my contention that he was shoved off," Walters argued. "They seen he had a few drinks in him and shoved him. They had no use for our fellers then."

And so *Bluenose* sailed for home — with her trophy, and with her flag at half-mast. She never did race *Mayflower*.

Wednesday — Noon Watch

After eight hours of rock-solid sleep, I feel human for the first time since we left Lunenburg. In the lounge the steward, Andrew Jones, offers me a bowl of wonderful chicken soup.

"You're in the third stage of seasickness," grins Don Barr. "In the first stage, you think you're going to die. In the second stage, you're afraid you might not die. In the third stage, you think you'd just as soon live."

"That's right."

"I've never been seasick on a ship," Barr reflects. "But I was nearly sick in a phone booth once. We'd just come in from sea, and that phone booth rocked and rolled like you wouldn't believe the moment I closed the door. I got out just in time."

"Well, I feel good enough to try that lasagna, Andrew."

But this is overconfidence, and I leave half the lasagna untouched. It will be another two days before my stomach is fully settled.

I go on deck into a world still bitterly cold and universally grey — grey sea, grey sky, and the grey forms of gulls and terns wheeling ceaselessly over the ocean. There is more life out here than a landsman might suppose. Other watches have seen whales and porpoises. Once or twice I see a gannet, and several times a brown and white bird passes nearby — a fulmar, I suspect. All around us are storm petrels, tiny birds skimming the water, rising over waves and coasting down into troughs, restless and twinkling. These little birds spend their entire lives at sea. Seamen call them "Mother Carey's chickens", a name derived from the Latin *Mater Cara*. In French they are still *les oiseaux de Notre Dame*, Our Lady's birds. Even the name petrel derives from the Italian *Petrello*, "Little Peter."

But the real life out here is just to starboard, and a few fathoms down: George's Bank, a sprawling undersea plateau rising to within nine feet of the surface in places, crowded with scallops, lobsters, and groundfish, shared by

Canadian and American fishermen for two centuries. *Blue-nose II* has passed three other banks — La Have, Baccaro, and Brown's — and has skirted the eastern edge of George's, turning west to 266 degrees magnetic just half an hour before our watch. We will steer along the southern fringe of George's Bank all day today, with trawlers working in the distance and only thirty or forty fathoms of water under our keel.

A bird flutters off the deckhouse and alights in the waterway — a canary of some kind, lime-yellow and black, with a mask around his eyes like a raccoon's. A little flycatcher or warbler, perhaps — a land bird, in any case, ruffled and blown about by the northwesterly wind. When a crewman approaches, the bird flutters away in panic, knocked this way and that by gusts off the sails and rigging. He alights on the ship again, looking tiny, frail, and cold. What is he doing out here, anyway, 180 miles from the nearest land?

"He'll be dead by morning," says Barr.

How come?

"They land aboard a ship and eat the salt crystals," Barr explains. "Must seem like food to them. And I guess all that salt kills them. Sometimes you'll find half a dozen of them dead on deck in the morning."

My trick at the wheel, a great bronze casting from the Lunenburg Foundry, studded with oaken spokes. *Bluenose II* is not particularly responsive. David Stevens, namesake and grandfather of my shipmate, who in his retirement makes a hobby of designing and building forty-five-foot schooners, steered both *Bluenoses* and found them "terrible sluggish" by comparison with his racing schooner *Kathi Anne II*. He's right. You have to anticipate the ship all the time. If you want her to move to port, you crank the wheel around, and wait. Then, as soon as she starts swinging, you crank it back, moving to stop the turn just as it commences. She has a rhythm of her own, too. She hangs right on course for some moments, then wanders away in a determined fashion. You have to turn that wheel hard to hold her on course.

The little warbler weakens noticeably as the watch goes on. By the time the watch ends the — wind rising, the sea tumbling — the bird scarcely moves when one approaches it, huddled in a coil of rope or tucked in between the racks of inflatable life rafts on the deckhouse roof. Sometime later that afternoon, it vanishes forever, a little bundle of yellow feathers bobbing in the wake, a morsel for a seal or a shark, a little life extinguished.

If the series of 1922 was an ill-tempered affair, that of 1923 was even worse. The next American contender was *Columbia* — in the view of Angus Walters and many others, the finest challenger of all. Like *Mayflower* and *Puritan*, she was designed by Starling Burgess. Like *Ford*, she was built by Arthur D. Story in Essex. She was 124 feet long with a 26-foot beam, and her sweeping lines bear some resemblance to those of *Bluenose* — a short, straight keel with a long, sweeping forefoot and overhanging bow, a sharply raked sternpost, and an even more steeply raked heart-shaped transom. A photograph of *Columbia* just after her launching reveals her to have been one of those ships so sweet in her lines, so well favoured in her bearing, as to seem slightly unreal, like something beyond the capability of mere men to create.

After the required season on the Banks, *Columbia* beat *Ford* easily in the American eliminations, and on October 27 a huge crowd greeted her as she swept into Halifax. Her skipper was Ben Pine, a Newfoundlander who had become a power in the New England fishing industry. By 1923 he was no longer a working fisherman, but Angus Walters, who knew him well, brushed this technicality aside. "He'll do fine," said Walters.

The first race was a splendid contest between two noble schooners and two expert skippers, battling side by side to a dead heat at the third mark. They swung onto the windward leg. Coming up to Bell Rock Buoys, *Columbia*, thirty feet to leeward of *Bluenose*, kept crowding in on the champion, forcing her right out of the channel and into shoal waters — and not just a sandbank either, but the Sambro

Ledges, a wasteland of rocks that has claimed dozens of vessels.

Henry Latter, the Halifax harbour pilot, shouted to Walters to bear away, that he was standing into danger.

"Bear away and we strike him!" yelled Long Albert Himmelman, at the helm.

"Strike him or strike the rocks!" cried Latter.

Walters shouted to Pine to give him room. Pine ignored the shout. The pilot called that he would no longer be responsible for the safety of the vessel.

"Pine, you can do as you like," Walters yelled. "I'm swinging and I'm swinging fast!"

Long Albert put the helm up and *Bluenose* swung away from the reefs. But her huge main boom caught *Columbia's* main rigging, slipped forward, and caught her fore rigging, slipped again, and caught her jibstay. For about a minute and a half *Bluenose* actually towed *Columbia*.

Then she broke free, and lunged for the finish line, crossing just eighty seconds ahead of *Columbia*. It was a near thing, but a decisive win.

Tempers flared. The rules of racing make it clear that no vessel has the right to put another on the rocks. At the same time, colliding with a competitor is equally illegal. Walters' only choice was somehow to slow his vessel and cross *behind Columbia*, almost certainly losing the race because of Pine's infraction. Neither skipper entered a protest — each, after all, was vulnerable to one — and the race went to *Bluenose*.

Nevertheless, the committee was incensed and to prevent repetition of the incident it made a ruling that all buoys were henceforth to be passed to seaward. It was a sensible ruling, designed to prevent real danger to vessels and crews. Pine and Walters were not consulted, however, and were simply notified by letter.

The next race was much like the first — a close battle between two well-matched vessels — but *Bluenose* led narrowly all the way, finishing two minutes and forty-five seconds ahead. What happened after that could reduce Walters to spluttering fury forty years later.

Bluenose, it was announced, had won the trophy, and a celebration banquet was held in the old Halifax Hotel. Pine and his crew were late arriving, and midway through the meal both skippers were called away to a committee meeting. There, Angus Walters learned that the committee had given the day's race to *Columbia*, setting the series at one all. The reason: *Bluenose* had passed a customs buoy on the wrong side. The buoy was not a course marker, not even a navigational buoy. It had been established to mark the point at which customs inspectors would board inbound ships.

Walters was furious. In the first place, the committee had no power to change the rules without the changes being acknowledged and accepted by the competitors. In the second place, his technical "infraction" had made no difference to the outcome of the race.

"Ben," he demanded, "did I gain or you lose anything by my passing that buoy on the side I did?"

"Oh, I don't know about that," Pine said.

Years later, Walters was still fuming. "I wouldn't have been so damn small as to accept a race I didn't win. Pine — I never met a better man, personally, but he let the committee rule him too much."

Walters made a counter-proposal: disregard the disputed race. "There's where Ben should have said, 'That's pretty square.' He didn't say a word. So I told them to go straight to hell and we left."

The next day Premier Murray came to Walters to try to change his mind. The little skipper was adamant. It's only a sport, said the premier. Yes, but it's damned hard work, replied Walters, you should come along as a member of the crew in the next race and find out. The premier declined. Arthur Zwicker, president of the Bluenose Schooner Company, began searching for another skipper and crew to race *Bluenose*. Walters got wind of this, put his gear aboard the ship, and cast off. Zwicker, apparently, had forgotten that Angus Walters was not only the skipper; he was also a major shareholder and managing director of the company. The Halifax tugboats, however, had been warned not to help *Bluenose* leave, and Walters couldn't get a tow from his berth.

"Then I see the water boat come by," Walters remembered. "Her name was good for what was to be. Name was *Defiance*." The engineer was from Lunenburg and he gave Walters a tow. As the committee watched, *Bluenose* vanished in the general direction of Lunenburg.

They told Pine he could have the trophy if he would simply sail over the course. Pine, to his credit, sailed out to the line and kept right on to Gloucester. This made him a hero in New England, a sharp contrast to the "poor sportsmanship" of Angus Walters. The heroism was less clear to Canadians, who could not see much difference between claiming one race on a technicality and claiming a series on the same basis. After much wrangling, the prize money was divided equally between the two vessels and the trophy stayed with *Bluenose*. Properly so, in Walters' opinion — his ship had raced *Columbia* twice and beaten her twice.

By now it was clear to everyone that Angus Walters and *Bluenose* were something out of the ordinary: a remarkable marriage of vessel and master. It was clear to the Halifax committee, too, that Walters was not their creature and could not be counted upon to obey their orders. They commissioned Bill Roue to design them another schooner, *Haligonian*, which they arranged to have built in Shelburne, specifically to beat *Bluenose*.

In the meantime it was clear to all hands that there was no profit or joy in racing when such bitter feelings were engendered and when the races were becoming as legalistic and fussy as the America's Cup. For the next eight years the trophy stayed in Lunenburg uncontested while *Bluenose* went fishing.

These were good years for *Bluenose*, bringing large catches and steady dividends. In 1926 she faced *Haligonian* off Halifax and whipped her soundly in two straight races. *Haligonian*'s owners never asked for a rematch, and she remains one of the great might-have-beens. Plenty of people still regret that *Haligonian* was never raced under a man like George Himmelman, who fished her from 1934 to 1938 and cared for her deeply.

"Great ships, all forgot," Capt. Himmelman said long afterward. "All forgot except the *Bluenose*. And I don't like that. All the young people hear is *Bluenose*. She was built in 1921 and there were a hundred and thirty schooners around here. Many, many of them were as good as the *Bluenose*."

But the schooners were disappearing and they were not being replaced. Two Lunenburgers, *Sadie E. Knickle* and *Sylvia Mosher*, were lost off Sable Island with all hands in 1926. *Henry Ford* was lost off Newfoundland in 1928. *Columbia*'s end was particularly chilling. On August 24, 1927, without warning, black clouds covered the sky and the wind struck at one hundred miles per hour. The sea erupted and the fishing fleet found itself fighting for survival. Back in Nova Scotia, orchards and buildings were being blown down and scores of vessels driven ashore.

Bluenose escaped with the loss of her anchors and fishing gear. But nearby, inside the sickle curve of Sable, four Lunenburg schooners went down — *Mahala, Clayton Walters, Uda A. Corkum,* and *Joyce M. Smith.* Eighty-five men were lost. And *Columbia,* riding at anchor with the Lunenburgers, went down, too, with her twenty-two men. The next day *Bluenose* sailed through the area and found the water littered with debris: broken dories, trawl tubs, oars.

Months later, on New Year's Day, after the memorial services and the mourning, the steam trawler *Venosta* was towing her steel-framed net in the area and found it fouled on some obstruction. Pulling hard to get clear, using full engine power and all their winches, the crewmen of *Venosta* were thunderstruck to see two mastheads break through the water behind them. Dripping with water, glistening in the pewter moonlight, a Banks schooner rose smoothly to the surface, rolling and pitching — but upright. There was no sign of any human being. The vessel looked sound. Even her rigging was largely intact, though she had no sails or booms.

The cable parted. The schooner dropped slowly below the waves again. But her classical, fluid lines had been as good as a signature.

Columbia. Hail and farewell.

Don Barr dreams of a big schooner paying her way by hauling cargo. Bill Lutwick has lovingly restored two daysailers. He has just sold a small schooner, and he and his brother plan to build another. They all want to know the details of the little cutter I am preparing to launch. Delbé Comeau was going to build a thirty-two-foot double-ender, and then he found a twenty-four-foot hard-chine sloop at a bargain-basement price, complete with engine, sails, and trailer. He bought her. Every spring he cleans her up, paints her, and makes her ready for the water. Then he leaves her on the trailer and spends the summer as second mate on *Bluenose II*. He gets home about the first of November, launches her, and sails her for two blustery weeks. He thinks he might trailer her south for the winter. But there have always been other opportunities. A couple of years ago, someone loaned Don Barr a racing sloop in the Bahamas, and Delbé took Mary to join the Barrs on a seven-week cruise.

Men who love boats can talk about them endlessly, comparing rigs and gadgets, refining the dream of the ultimate boat, measuring fiberglass and steel against wood and epoxy. The crew of *Bluenose II* passes many a pleasant watch ruminating on such topics. Given a little prompting, every member of the permanent crew will admit he thinks himself incredibly fortunate to be paid for doing something he would gladly do for nothing.

Such a career, of course, presents some problems. For one thing, there is no possibility of advancement. Countries like Ecuador, Chile, Mexico, and Romania can afford to own square-riggers to train seamen for the navy and the merchant marine. Norway and the United States each have several tall ships. Canada evidently cannot afford one. In Canada, one little province has one splendid schooner, descendant of a mythic fleet, and we are aboard her, talking through the night, as the lights of fishing boats on George's Bank approach, pass, and fall astern.

The trawlers on the horizon, methodically sweeping the surface of the bank with their great open-mouthed nets, are also descended from the schooners. Each in its day represented the most economical means of gathering fish. The saltbanking fleet made three or four trips a year, gutting and splitting the catch and salting it down in the hold. Once she "had her salt wet," the ship sailed home, unloaded the fish she had caught over the last couple of months, and sailed again for the Banks. Once anchored on the grounds, the crew set out in dories before daylight anchoring long lines of trawl with baited hooks every fathom or so and working back and forth along them until late at night. Dorymen hauled the line over one side of the boat, removing fish and rebaiting hooks, and dropped the line back over the opposite side. When the dory was full, the dorymen rowed back to the schooner to unload. When the weather was bad, the men stayed aboard the ship. When the fishing was poor in one location, the ship moved to another.

Fishing has always built powerful links between fishermen, who depend on one another for their lives and their livelihoods, and dory fishing has a certain romance for those of us who never did it; but, says one old doryman, it was "a disgustin' job. A fearful disgustin' job." All this brutal labour might bring a return of as little as a hundred dollars for a season, and when the fish were running, a doryman could work seventy-two hours straight.

Every year in Lunenburg there is a memorial service for the men lost at sea that year. Angus Walters' papers include the programme for every memorial service from the 1920s to Walters' death in 1968, and reading through them is appalling: scores and scores of men lost in dories in the fog and snow, men swept overboard, schooners sunk with all hands. Today's huge steel draggers are cold, featureless machines, and the fishing grounds cannot forever stand up to their scouring, but nobody in his senses would want to go back to schooners and dories, however lovely the ships may have been.

In the history of ships, it often happens that the most glorious development of a type occurs just as economics and technology are conspiring to drive that type from the seas altogether. The towering steel square-riggers that carried grain and wool from Australia to England in the early years of this century were, perhaps, the most magnificent sailing vessels of all time — marvels of design, fast and strong and able, capable of hauling enormous cargoes with a handful of men as crew. When steamers and sailing vessels were travelling the oceans together, the wind ships often beat the steamers, port to port. But the steamers were reliable and, as they developed, ultimately faster. So, too, in the fishery. By 1920, when the International races began, says Howard Chapelle, "the sailing schooner was obsolete."

She was, indeed, and so was her whole style of fishing. The schooners competed for many years by installing engines, fishing in the winter, shortening their masts, and using their sails essentially as steadying devices and as occasional aids during favourable winds. A number of vessels were built, in fact, to this hybrid style, including the Lunenburg museum ship *Theresa E. Connor*, launched in 1938. Many of the older schooners were converted. F. W. Wallace tells us that John Apt was contemplating the installation of an engine in the *Albert J. Lutz* as early as 1913 when he inspected the new auxiliary schooner *Bay State* in Canso Harbour. Gordon Thomas reports that the last pure sailing schooner in Gloucester was launched in 1905. At length, even the auxiliaries gave way to pure motor vessels. Gloucester's last dory schooner gave up in 1953. In Lunenburg the schooners hung on for another decade, but in 1963 the last skipper of the *Theresa E. Connor* could not assemble enough dorymen, even in Newfoundland, to make a trip. Dory fishing was finished forever.

The pivotal year was 1930. The market for salt fish had been shrinking for years. Now, with an international depression, the countries of the Caribbean and southern Europe could not afford even six cents a pound. There was a market for fresh and frozen fish, but that market was in the eastern United States — a long way from Nova Scotia. To get fresh fish to Boston, fishermen needed small, fast, engine-powered vessels. The big saltbankers were suddenly irrelevant. *Bluenose* kept working, but never again made enough money to cover more than her own expenses. Eventually she could not even do that.

Angus Walters stayed ashore in 1930, and his brother John took *Bluenose* to Newfoundland for bait. On June 13, following a pilot's orders, "Sonny" Walters ran her ashore on the gravel beach at Argentia. There she lay for four days, grinding sand into her bilges, until the government steamer *Arras* was able to pull her free. She was nine years old now, heavy with absorbed water, and after the grounding she needed between one and ten tons of extra ballast in her starboard bilge. She was hastily repaired in Burin, Newfoundland, and as a result she handled clumsily.

At this point, Ben Pine came to Nova Scotia and challenged Angus Walters to race a brand-new schooner, *Gertrude L. Thebaud*, launched the previous year. Walters declined. *Bluenose* was in no shape to race, and her owners could not afford to put her in shape.

Pine persisted. Sir Thomas Lipton had put up a trophy and a cash prize. In the end Angus agreed. He had a new suit of sails cut and made a record passage to Gloucester. *Bluenose* was poorly tuned, having fished to the last moment, and the swift run down the coast had stretched her new sails out of shape.

"I found I didn't have the *Bluenose*," Walters said. "I had some other boat. My God, if I may say so, she was in hard shape. She should never have been asked to race." He could hardly induce her to tack. In the first race, on October 9, she lost by fifteen minutes. In the following days, the schooners started twice again, and twice the race was called off for lack of wind. In the meantime, Ben Pine had fallen ill and been replaced by Charley Johnson, while *Bluenose* had made some quick repairs to her damaged keel and recut her sails.

On October 15, a raw, rainy day, the second race began
— only to be called off because the committee decided the
schooners could not find the buoys that marked the turns.
Walters was furious. *Bluenose* had been leading by two
miles, and if they couldn't race in light winds or heavy
winds, when could they race?

The second race was finally held on October 18. The
wind was light and baffling, but *Bluenose* took an early lead
and at the eighteen-mile mark was five minutes ahead.

Then Angus Walters made the worst blunder of his
whole racing career, as he himself admitted. Instead of
staying with *Thebaud* and blanketing her sails, he split tacks
with her and headed inshore looking for a favourable slant
of wind. He found less wind and from a less helpful direction. *Thebaud* took full advantage of the error and crossed
the finish line eight minutes ahead, winning the series.

Angus Walters was enraged by his own stupidity. On
the way in, the American observer aboard could see Walters was heading for a reef and didn't have the courage to
tell him. "He was so mad he was ready to throw someone
over," said the observer. Walters hit the reef, which only
made him madder. He was indignant on behalf of his ship
and angry with himself for letting her down. "*Thebaud*
didn't beat *Bluenose*!" he protested. "She beat me!"

A confident Ben Pine called for a new series for the
International Trophy. The return match was held the following year off Halifax. *Bluenose* was leading the first race
by thirty-five minutes when the six-hour time allowance
expired. Two days later *Bluenose* won by thirty-two minutes. *Thebaud* was handling badly — her sails ill-fitting, her
ballast too heavy. The following day *Thebaud* handled better, but *Bluenose* whipped by her again, finishing twelve
minutes ahead. A smug and saucy Angus Walters re-
marked that *Bluenose* had been lonely during the races,
Thebaud being so far behind. Though he had admired several other American challengers, Walters had no use for
Thebaud. He called her a "shoofly" and a "toy" and claimed
Ben Pine had been afraid to tack her in any kind of breeze
for fear of capsizing her.

The two were to meet in one final series seven years later. Meanwhile, both were caught in the malaise of the fishery. In 1933 Ben Pine loaded a delegation of fishermen and fish dealers aboard *Thebaud* and sailed her down to Washington to discuss the industry's crisis with President Roosevelt. Four years later, Angus Walters became president of a fishing union that tied up Lunenburg and Halifax, seeking a quarter-cent per pound increase in the price of fish. He was characteristically blunt about the demand.

"The dealers say they can't afford to pay more for fish," he cried. "I ask them, did not fish bring them wealth? Dealers always argue that it was a poor year. I ask them how they can buy up vessels and draggers at the cost of hundreds of thousands of dollars? I'd like to ask some of them who complain most loudly how much money their fathers left them — money that was made by the sweat of the men who sailed to the Banks."

The union made some gains, but it would be another forty years before fishermen would begin to receive the kind of money they deserved. In the meantime, *Bluenose* was trying all manner of tricks to make a dollar. In 1933 her hold was stripped and cabins were installed to starboard, while to port she was fitted with models and exhibits showing the Banks fishery. Thus equipped, she sailed up the St. Lawrence and into the Great Lakes, visiting Toronto and other ports en route to the World's Fair at Chicago. In Chicago she was chartered — and sued by the charterers; she accompanied a yacht race; she found a bullet-riddled body dumped off the wharf just astern of her; and she was investigated and charged with various customs infractions. By the time *Bluenose* slipped her lines, Angus Walters must have felt the North Atlantic to be a haven of safety compared to Chicago.

Then followed the transatlantic voyage to the Royal Jubilee and, in 1936, the melancholy but inevitable decision to install engines.

"I knew damn well I was ruining the *Bluenose*," Walters conceded. "But what the hell could I do? I didn't see why I should piss around in the fog when the others weren't and not do so well as plenty of 'em who weren't so good fishermen as me.

"We raced again and we won, but we shouldn't have. *Bluenose* wasn't half the boat she had been. We had put all that damn iron and concrete into her. It killed her."

It killed her economically, too, saddling her with a seven-thousand-dollar debt she was never able to pay. She was wholly obsolete now, lurching from fishing trips to exhibitions, running charter cruises out of Halifax, desperately paying interest on the loan for her engines. Her gear was run-down. She needed paint. She was a national myth loved by millions who would never see her, and she was all but a ruin by 1938.

Ironically, her image appeared in 1937 on, of all things, the nation's money. The mint has never admitted that the "Fishing Schooner Under Full Sail" on the Canadian dime is *Bluenose*, but all Canadians know her. Look at the lift of that bow, the thrust of that proud bowsprit. What other fishing schooner could it possibly be? What other schooner has earned the right to be a national emblem?

Finally, in 1938, the challenge came again. Would *Bluenose* race *Thebaud*, just one last time?

Angus Walters wavered. His beloved ship was old, heavy, and shabby. It would take ten thousand dollars to put her in shape, and where was he to find ten thousand dollars? He was a widower of fifty-six, secretly engaged to a young Halifax woman named Mildred Butler, and he was looking for employment ashore — as harbour master of Halifax, for instance. Two years later he started a dairy where he worked for the rest of his life.

But *Bluenose* weighed on him. He wanted to see her preserved in honour: berthed in concrete behind his home on the Lunenburg waterfront, perhaps, and open to tourists. All those men, all those schooners, that had made Lunenburg rich and captured the imagination of a nation — was there to be no memorial to any of them? Had it meant nothing? Hardly anyone — individual, town, corporation, government — was willing to consider spending the little it would take to give an honourable retirement to a national symbol.

The Americans, it turned out, were willing to promise eight-thousand dollars to *Bluenose*, to prepare her for racing. Until she was beaten, after all, Gloucester would chafe at being second-best. The federal department of fisheries finally came across with another $2,500 and the province contributed $1,000. Even this was not enough. Doug Pyke, who was working with his father, took the summer off to sail with Walters, helping to organize harbour tours and souvenir sales in Halifax to raise money. Later in New England, when money again ran short, Pyke collected all the Canadian dimes he could lay his hands on, called them "silver engraving souvenirs of the *Bluenose*," and hawked them in Boston and Gloucester for $2 each.

Bluenose sailed into Gloucester October 2, 1938, looking like a queen again. This time the series was to consist of five races sailed over short courses near the shore off both Boston and Gloucester, and there were to be no restrictions on sails, crew, or ballast. Walters objected to these provisions, which were contrary to the Deed of Gift, and the whole series was disfigured by much wrangling and bickering, accusations and acrimony.

On October 9, *Bluenose* led to the first mark, lost the lead on the second leg, took it back again on the windward leg, and was outmaneuvered by Ben Pine on the final run. Soon after Pine took the lead, Walters was forced to reduce sail. His bowsprit, weakened by an accident in Lunenburg, had cracked. Most accounts say it was the fore-topmast; Doug Pyke has photographs to back up his recollection that it was the bowsprit. Its replacement was turned on a huge lathe in a Boston shipyard. But its loss made no real difference. *Thebaud* had the race won before the accident.

"It was a grand race," said Angus. "You know two boats can't win, and Ben sure knows how to sail."

The second race was postponed twice. When it was finally sailed, the two skippers swapped the lead several times before *Bluenose* pulled decisively ahead to win by eleven

minutes. The Gloucester men entered a protest. *Bluenose,*
they claimed, was too long on the waterline.

They were right. She had been launched with seventy
tons of ballast but she was now so logy and low that she
carried only fifty. Despite this, her waterline was found to
be 114 feet. Walters had already removed her engines.
Now he removed fuel tanks and generator. While she was
being measured, he kept the crew below. When the measurers were at the bow, the crew walked to the stern, raising the bow. When the measurers went aft, the crew went
forward. Walters also kept a pile of extra ballast on the
wharf. When the forecast called for strong winds, the crew
secretly loaded the extra ballast. When light winds were
expected, they unloaded it. The opposition found out
about this and sprinkled sand over the ingots of ballast,
leaving the imprint of them clearly on the wharf as evi-
dence to support a protest.

It was not a game, this series. Both sides were grimly
determined to win. When I asked Doug Pyke about the
mobile ballast, he said, "Let's just say that if there was
anything like that going on, it was not confined to any one
boat." Gloucester knew perfectly well that this was the last
series, the last chance to defeat *Bluenose.* Angus Walters
knew it too, and he was determined to win — not for
money, not for himself, but for his ship. "The *Bluenose* was
a living thing to Angus," Pyke says. "She was not just
something built of wood." He loved her as a man may love
a woman. Until she was properly at rest, there could be no
rest for him — and perhaps if she could thrash the Yanks
just once more, a grateful Canada would put her to rest in
dignity.

The controversy over her waterline helped her in the
end. Lightened, she was noticeably faster and handier. But
the next race was postponed five times, during which
Thebaud was three times hauled out for paint and repairs.
On October 21, Cecil Moulton — skippering *Thebaud* in
place of the ailing Ben Pine — protested that *Bluenose* had
taken on ballast the previous night. He was right no doubt,
but the committee would brook no further delays. As it

turned out, the extra ballast was a disadvantage. The wind was light, and *Thebaud*, with a topmast hand named Sterling Hayden, took a substantial lead before the breeze died altogether, cancelling the race. But *Thebaud*, Walters charged, had also violated the rule by adding a new, large jib.

Finally, on October 23, *Bluenose* won a luffing match early in the race and sailed on to a six-minute victory, only to lose the fourth race the following day when a backstay broke, endangering the rig and the lives of the two men clinging to the whipping spars. *Bluenose* luffed up and a temporary backstay was quickly rove. But *Thebaud* was gone.

The last race of the series, the last race *Bluenose* ever sailed, began at 12:04 on October 26. A single race which brought so many things to a focus — the series, the proud record of *Bluenose* and her men, the Canadian standard which the Americans had never met, the terrible and magnificent history of the schooner fishery, and the end of sail itself as a workingman's way of life. Angus Walters looked up at the spars, the rigging, the clouds of sail. He listened to the old vessel creaking, felt the rise and fall of her well-worn decks. Something had broken lately almost every time he had pushed her.

Could she win, just once more?

Could he bear it if she lost?

The starting gun cracked. *Thebaud* was already close to the starting line.

"Come on, you long black bitch!" shouted Angus.

Before the first mark, *Bluenose* had surged past *Thebaud*. No question about it, the old girl was going like an express train. The two vessels swung around the first mark broad-reaching for the second. *Bluenose* was still pulling ahead. She was leading by four minutes at the next buoy. Then she swung a little wide and *Thebaud* made a neat turn, and the two were into a fierce duel, tacking side by side up the nine-mile windward leg. Angus Walters was taut as a rigging wire himself, every nerve and muscle willing the schooner forward. And yes, she was gaining ground again —

"One more time, old girl!" Angus pleaded. "Just one more time!"

With a crack like a pistol shot, a topsail halyard block broke. The sail could no longer be tacked. Angus Walters looked around. It didn't matter. Even without that topsail, *Bluenose* was too far ahead to be caught.

With her rail dipping towards the water, half her foresail wet with spray, *Bluenose* sprinted for the finish. She had never sailed better, never sailed faster. She was setting a record, in fact. No vessel in the history of sail had ever covered a fixed course so fast — 14.15 knots, average, on all points of sailing, over the forty miles.

The great black schooner from Canada stormed across the line two minutes and fifty seconds ahead of her rival — an awesome sight, a legendary ship at the moment of her final and greatest triumph. The crowd was silent for a moment. And then the bells and whistles and horns of Boston burst on the air, mingling with the cheers of crews and crowds alike in a thunderous ovation.

She had won the regard of a foreign city. She had won the race, the series, and the trophy.

And she would keep them forever.

Thursday — Graveyard Watch

Struggling into my sailing suit, I reflect that a ship at sea really does become an independent mini-world, with its own rituals, its own priorities, even its own time. Days cease to mean anything. Time is measured in watches. Sometime after four each morning, I go to bed, sleeping till almost midday. Noon brings a four-hour watch, then eight hours of writing, reading, talking, eating, napping. Then the night watch again.

The sky is clear and high, dusted with stars and floodlit by a full moon, its cold path brilliant on the face of the drowsy sea. The ocean is never still. It is one thing to say this, another to experience it: anytime, day or night, winter or summer, in Homer's time or ours, the wine-dark sea is never still. No matter when you come on deck, the ocean is moving. The schooner breathes her way across the waters, rising and falling like the chest of a sleeper. Her rhythm recalls the five men I have left below in the hold, sprawled across their canted berths, blankets gathered around them, mouths open, eyelids fluttering — strong, muscular young men in the prime of their bodily lives, but in their sleep somehow even more poignant and vulnerable than children.

Bluenose II is jogging along under foresail and jumbo, close south of Little George's Bank, in twenty to thirty fathoms of water. We are steering 270 degrees, the sails sheeted flat to a light southwesterly breeze, the engines turning industriously. It is a meditative, reflective night of soft conversation and philosophic silences. I lie on my back on the deckhouse, watching the spreaders raking the sky, the boom and gaff captured by tackles and chains hold the mainsail imprisoned between them. The boom is a gift of Macmillan Bloedel, carried from British Columbia to Nova Scotia gratis by the CNR — a huge length of Douglar fir, or "Oregon pine" as shipwrights often call it, with a plaque on it to record the gratitude of the provincial government for this corporate generosity. Nova Scotia once had immense trees like these, but even in the time of the original *Bluenose* they had been cut and exported in the form of laths, lumber, timbers, and ships. British Columbians should examine the stubby spruce forests that now blanket the Maritimes, and pay more attention to the future than we did. Nova Scotia was the richest province in Canada in 1867, and its prosperity was built on huge trees, now vanished.

Bluenose II requires two full miles of rope for her running rigging, not to mention the wire standing rigging that keeps the masts in her. The main peak halyard itself is a whole six-hundred-foot coil of inch-thick polyester braid. The afterdeck is a pleasant place to be, this evening, waiting for one's trick at the wheel and surveying the ship's appearance.

The boys are laughing about "eating at the Gig Ho Ho," this having been an evening when the cook, Noble Gignac, known as "Gigs," offered Chinese food. Gigs is a short, grey, bearded veteran of twenty-five years in the galleys of the navy, a friendly but quiet native of the French enclave around Windsor, Ontario. Despite his name, he speaks not a word of French. Never has. When he serves Italian food, the galley becomes the Gignarini. One of his most memorable dishes is rabbit chow mein, invented one night after Bill Lutwick ran over a rabbit while driving his old pickup down from Halifax. Bill was upset about this, but Rick Moore was amused. He picked up the flat rabbit and heaved it into the back of the truck.

Aboard the ship, the rabbit became the focus of a jovial evening. The boys took photos of it wearing sunglasses, smoking a cigarette, staring in horror as a crewman threatened to open his fly. Finally they skinned it and put it in the fridge. Next day, it vanished into the Gig Ho Ho. Murray Stevens, David's father, was aboard for lunch the next day. Rabbit chow mein. He took it very well.

Bluenose II is now older than *Bluenose* was at the time of her last race and she has stories of her own. Her life falls into four periods. The first covers the enthusiasm that led up to her launching on July 24, 1963, through her assignment as host ship at Expo '67. Then she suffered a period of uncertainty and neglect, during which she was given to the province by the Oland family, whose brewery had built her. The third period was sheer Gilbert and Sullivan, as the government tried to decide whether she was a yacht for the cabinet, a useful avenue for patronage, a sailing ambassador, a tour ship, or a floating museum. Finally, in the Brown-Barr regime, she has evolved into a well-managed public relations vehicle with a clearly defined role and a set of competent managers who deeply respect her dignity.

By the end of the watch, the sky has clouded over, leaving us in a faint luminescence of diffused moonlight. Charlie goes below to awaken the next watch. Wayne Walters comes on deck wearing his heavy watch jacket and wool toque. He consults with Delbé Comeau about the ship's position and the conditions during the last four hours. Our watch straggles below.

It has not been easy for Wayne, a seaman who is the grandson of the most famous fisherman in the world. "People always ask, *Do you remember your grandfather?*" he says "Well, of course I remember my grandfather. We were in the same family. *What was he like?* As a matter of fact, we hated each other's guts. He called me a lazy little good-for-nothing so-and-so. But that's not what they want to hear. You're supposed to tell 'em that he took you on his knee and told you all these great stories and filled your baby bottle with dark rum. You were born in a dory and your mother rowed to Sable Island and back for the exercise before she brought you home."

He speaks softly, a man of thirty-five with a penetrating gaze and a sense of humour that slides fast ones past you before you notice. He may look at the chart and compare it with the forecast and develop a set of hypotheses. If one low-pressure system passes north, and another stalls in the Great Lakes, and a third fails to develop, then we can expect comfortable weather and favourable winds. Somewhere in this extrapolation he has passed from reasonable projections to wishful thinking, and as he realizes this himself he says, without so much as a flicker of expression,

"And the hands could all get laid, too, within ten minutes of docking at Atlantic City. It's just as likely."

He is a good raconteur. The sea breeds storytellers, men who can make a long watch pass quickly, and this ship abounds in them. Wayne tells, for example, about signing aboard a Florida-bound yacht in New York. The owner thought Wayne and his buddy had money, and they thought the owner had money. In fact everyone was broke and they came close to starving before the trip was finished. The owner had had half his stomach removed because of ulcers and his notion of a meal was "a slice of bread with a little canned meat spread on it — canned spasm, I call it — just enough to discolour the bread." They pulled into one harbour in the fog with a single slice of bread left. While the others went into town, Wayne used the slice of bread to lure a flock of tame ducks. When they were close enough, he drew a pellet pistol and shot a duck in the head at point-blank range. The other ducks took off, pattering and squawking. The victim had been deranged but not killed, and it accelerated across the harbour, paddling furiously and erratically. A nearby yacht had a Zodiac inflatable with an outboard, and in three quick shouts Wayne promised the neighbour a share of the soup if he would help catch the duc... The two of them jumped into the Zodiac and went careening around the misty harbour at high speed, trying to overtake the frantic fowl. At length they overhauled it and Wayne reached over the side, knife at the ready, wrenched the duck aboard by its neck, and instantly slashed its throat. Then he looked up. Above him was a highway bridge crowded with people, all watching.

Wayne is almost serious in his caustic view of Angus. The old man was eighty when Wayne went to work at the dairy where Angus was still showing up at four-thirty every morning and "humping sixty-pound milk cans, and I could hardly keep up with him. He hadn't accepted that things had changed since he was a boy and you went to work at twelve or thirteen and worked all year for two cents a pound. But I was very much the junior member of the family — the son of the youngest son — and nobody wanted to hear my opinion, ever. The warmest thing my grandfather ever said to me was after I had joined the navy. He said, 'Come up to the house and have a drink of rum, boy.'"

Wayne stayed three years in the navy. He has twice been hired on *Bluenose II* without reference to his grandfather, a fact which pleases him. In 1973 he was serving on gypsum boats plying from Nova Scotia to the eastern United States. He went to visit a friend aboard *Bluenose II* and was immediately hired as second mate, though he had no ticket and wasn't looking for a job.

"Those were the real old hard-core days. You wore what you liked, had your hair down to your shoulders, and kept a forty-ounce bottle of black rum in the fo'c'sle. If you didn't feel too good in the morning, you took a shot of that and a glass of water. Cap'n Skoje didn't care, as long as you did your work. In those days they kept the crew on the payroll all winter. We had a big shed on the wharf in Halifax where the crew overhauled the gear. The winter I was there, we did that, and drank fifty cases of beer and did a motor job on a Volkswagen as well. You'd take a game of checkers and go up on the spreaders and refuse to come down. When someone up there had to take a leak, you'd see these streams arching out into the light.... I stayed a year and a half that time."

After that, Wayne served several years on the oceanographic schooner *Vema*, travelling all over the Pacific and Indian oceans, gaining a practical education in navigation and seamanship, learning how to handle a vessel with scientific precision. He now holds a master's home trade ticket and has been back aboard *Bluenose II* since 1978. Last December he won a sailing master's endorsement on his ticket. Such an endorsement was still technically possible — "it was on the books" — but since World War II nobody had been granted one, and it took pressure on Ottawa to be allowed to sit for the endorsement. In the end he was examined on fore-and-aft rig by Ellsworth Coggins and a regular Department of Transport examiner. One of these days Don Barr is likely to embark on some unspeakably

improbable new adventure, and when Nova Scotia comes
to select a new master for *Bluenose II*, it will be hard to
decline the youngest qualified sailing master in Canada,
with years of experience aboard the ship he would like to
command.

And the fact that he is Angus Walters' grandson will be
the least of his qualifications. You don't call Wayne Walters
a lazy little good-for-nothing so-and-so and get away with
it — not even if you're the fabled Cap'n Angus.

Wayne is proud of his grandfather all the same, and he
shares some qualities with him. He doesn't shout — nobody
shouts aboard *Bluenose II*. Tourists have been known to
complain that they expected roaring skippers and hard-
case mates, but Barr does everything with nods and hand
signals. When Wayne gives an order, however, it is obeyed.
Right now.

Once, years ago, a tourist boarded the ship and began to
scream insults at Capt. Skoje. Wayne Walters was offended.
He believes that The Office of The Captain deserves respect. He stepped in front of the tourist and said he
thought the fellow had best be going. The tourist ignored
him. Wayne repeated the suggestion. When the tourist continued, Wayne lost his temper. He picked the man up and
threw him the width of the deck, and while the man scrambled for the gangway, Wayne snatched a hefty
stainless-steel belaying pin from the pinrail — "I knew
which one was loose" — and went for him, roaring with
fury. The man shot up the dock as though the hounds of
hell were after him, which they were. "I had it in mind to
beat his head in," Wayne says, chuckling softly at the mu-
tual folly. "I chased him halfway up Hollis Street."

Angus Walters would recognize that quality. He would
also recognize Wayne's stubborn determination. After
Bluenose won her final victory in 1938, Canada continued
to ignore her. So did the Bluenose Schooner Company and
its shareholders. They still owed seven thousand dollars on
her engines. They were unable to pay it as a company,
unwilling to do so as individuals. Fairbanks-Morse began
legal proceedings to seize the ship and sell her at auction.

Bluenose

Bluenose *in photographs by Angus MacAskill.*

Peter Brown did not like to be described as "a cheerful, round-faced, sandy-haired man with the best job in the world," even though that is exactly what he is.

Bluenose II *on the slip. Those long flowing lines are what give the ship her speed.*

Delbé Comeau was almost in despair when he joined the ship, believing that he would never find an occupation that would satisfy him for the rest of his life.

When Noble Gignac – "Gigs" – serves Italian food, his galley is the Gignarini. Once, in the Gig Ho Ho, he made rabbit chow mein.

The sun pours down on Don Barr, his feet spread wide on his quarterdeck, a broad and michievous smile splitting his open, happy face.

Bluenose II *requires two full miles of rope for her running rigging, not to mention the wire standing rigging that keeps the masts in her.*

Chief Engineer Ron Ottens: "The crew on this ship will pitch right in to help the engineer. There aren't too many crews like that."

The ship herself seems to have become animate, a loyal, intimate, trustworthy fellow adventurer.

There is something particularly poignant about a ship's departure, a faint aroma of death and high adventure. More than a thousand Lunenburgers have died at sea.

The crew lines up along the main boom, on top of the deckhouse, heaving the stiff fabric into some semblance of a furl.

The wine-dark sea is never still. The schooner breathes her way across the waters, rising and falling like the chest of a sleeper.

And so the schooner sets out, with her young, ardent crew.

We are a privileged few, those of us who have handled the wheel of a Banks schooner under a full press of sail, those who have come so near to the heart of a great legend of our country.

Nobody — not the government, not the fishing companies, not the town — made a move to help her. Angus Walters was heartsick and angry.

"They just couldn't see any personal profit in it," he said. "All the honour *Bluenose* brought to Canada, brought to the town, all the money the fishermen put in their pockets — why, they all got rich off the fishing fleet. They could have fixed her up so's people could understand the sort of work they done, what kind of character it took to build a champion...."

But nobody cared. Nobody but Angus Walters. And so, on the morning of the Saturday that she was to be auctioned Angus went to see the manager of the local bank. Before the auctioneer could raise his hammer, Angus Walters had put down his life's savings, even the proceeds of his life insurance, and taken over her debt himself.

Bluenose fished a little and freighted a little during the next three years, her bowsprit gone, her towering masts cut down, a blocky wheelhouse on her stern. Keeping her was a sentimental self-indulgence on Angus Walters' part, and he knew it. He tried valiantly to have her preserved, and by 1942 he knew he had failed. The West Indies Trading Company offered to buy her for use as a freighter carrying rum and sugar and bananas between the Caribbean islands.

He cast off her lines himself. "There was a lump in my throat. I knew it was good-bye, and she was like part of me. To tell you the goddamn truth, when I walked home, I felt like coming out of the cemetery." There were more tears to come. On January 29, 1946, at about nine-thirty in the evening, *Bluenose* struck LaFalle Reef off the port of Aux Cayes, Haiti, and sank. Angus Walters was called out of the curling rink and told she was gone. He cried. So did Jack Pardy, his helmsman in the 1938 races. So did many others. The *Halifax Herald*, which had so much to do with her creation, wrote her epitaph: "Her passing is a national sorrow; the ignominy of her death a national disgrace."

Thursday — Noon Watch

At six o'clock this morning, Wayne Walters took *Bluenose II* past Nantucket Lightship, the last of these floating light-houses that once marked major landfalls and dangers all along the Atlantic Coast. North of the lightship are patches of shoal and rock which look nasty even on the chart: Asia Rip, Phelps Bank, the Rose and Crown. There was no wind at all, just an oily swell as the schooner passed slowly three miles from the lightship, 210 miles east of New York City.

Now, at noon, she is steering 260 degrees, a little south of west, sixty-five miles from Martha's Vineyard. The sun floods down from an utterly blue sky. The water sparkles. A dragger works slowly in the middle distance. The wind is a gentle southeasterly. The jib has been raised to catch it. The visibility is not less than eight miles. The crewmen are stripped to the waist and some are in shorts. For the first time since we left Lunenburg, it is possible to do some maintenance work — run a roller thinly coated with black paint over the marks where she chafed the wharf, scour the white pawprints of a shipwright's dog off the deck where he walked after investigating some wet paint, caulk along the deckhouse where water has been seeping into Rick's and Delbé's cabins. Wayne Walters polishes brass. Jeff Steeve paints the covering board blue to match the deck-house. Gordon Powers and David Stevens work with Rick Moore setting up the rigging by taking the slack out of the lanyards. In a short-sleeved white shirt, Don Barr is in a talkative cheerful mood.

"I get fed up with the idea that this ship is only an illusion. Tourists ask you what happened to the 'real' one. And people go on about the way the old fellows did things. But if you asked the old fellows to go to sea with a crew of twelve instead of thirty, and with eight of those picked up out of school, never been to sea before, they'd say you were out of your tree. This ship ought to be 'real' enough for anyone.

"For the government, mind you, what we're doing here, going to sea, is incidental. The job of the ship is P.R., an there's no P.R. going on here. If they could *mail* the ship to Atlantic City, Canada Post, in two days, that would suit their purposes a lot better."

Barr says all this with a grin. His equanimity is astonishing. How many of us could take three hundred tourists a day in and out of Halifax Harbour for two solid months, answering the same questions, telling the same stories, gently dealing with the same forms of ignorance? And if we could, could we also sail the ship, deal with the vagaries of political direction, maintain an admirable *esprit de corps*, and break in eight green hands every time we took the ship on a voyage? Barr makes it look easy. Few qualified captains could do it at all.

"By the time these kids get back, they'll be changed," Barr is saying. "It's hard to put your finger on it, but they'll be different — more self-confident, better at meeting people. My neighbours in Indian Point, now, are like many, many Nova Scotians. In the run of a week, many of them don't speak to anyone they haven't known all their lives. In the next six weeks, these kids will meet more strangers than those people would meet in a lifetime. They'll have seen places those people will never see. And it'll change them. It always does."

It certainly will. One of the young men on deck right now is known as Forty-three, and the story behind his nickname makes Barr's point. *Bluenose II* generates nicknames — Lobo (short for Lobotomy), Tattoo (because Rick Moore evokes a character in TV's *Fantasy Island*), Porky, Rattler, the Kentville Cowboy, Yoda. The two girls who sell harbour tour tickets are Ticklet and Ticklet II. Their male associate is Boy Tickie.

Forty-three is the younger brother of Forty-two. Forty-two was a stripling who boarded the ship virginal in every sense. He did not smoke, did not drink, did not swear, and knew about women only by rumour. The crew diligently applied themselves to the enlargement of his understanding. They told him how to swear, but he had trouble getting the rhythm and flavour of it. They poured liquor into him and gave him cigarettes. They invited him to parties at which women would be present.

Then one night a girl at a party led him off into the woods. He returned to the ship at five in the morning, rowing a dinghy he had taken without its owner's consent and singing at the top of his lungs. The girl had done predictable things to him. He was a changed man. His voice deepened and his swearing developed resonance and timbre. He grew a beard and drank rum.

It had been his Summer of '42.

Late in the afternoon, we get into stories about the *Hilda Gerard*. One of the jobs Barr did to make a little money was to rig the square-rigged ship *Flying Cloud*, built in Meteghan for American owners in the early 1960s. When Barr worked on her, she was in Salem, Massachusetts, and she was about to fall victim to the Jones Act, which says that passengers may not be carried from one U.S. port to another except in U.S.-built ships. *Flying Cloud* is now an exhibit at Historic Gardener's Basin in Atlantic City, where Barr and I will look at her sorrowfully in a couple of days' time — her three lofty masts fallen, her bulwarks caving in with rot, beached in a shallow pond as a melancholy decoration in a seaside park.

But years ago, when she was rigged, she was towed out of Salem in a fog with one of Barr's crewmen aboard. Toby MacGregor was a huge man, with a halo of copper hair and a vast red beard, and the towline was so long that the tug could not be seen. *Flying Cloud* hove out of the mist right beside a startled sports fisherman. A coppery apparition drew himself up above the rail and demanded:

"You fellers see anything of a white whale hereabouts?"

Then she vanished in the mist.

Barr roars with laughter. The story reminds him of the time *Hilda Gerard* herself came to a wharf in Grand Manan Island, that remote and lovely outpost in the Bay of Fundy, and a good number of villagers appeared to watch her berth. Once the lines were secured, there was a moment of silence. Another crewman, a quiet little TV producer from Toronto, looked up at the crowd on the wharf and snarled: "Deliver us all your virgins — or we'll burn the town."

Barr laughs again. These are the times he lives for, out at sea, making a voyage, doing something worthy with this marvellous vessel. He looks around at this warm and welcome day and decides it is a good opportunity for some sail drill. We could set topsails. The crew has done this only once, and we may well wish to set all sail going into Atlantic City in the Parade of Sail Saturday.

Bluenose II is so well proportioned that one forgets how big she really is. Rick Moore and Ian Morrison go up the foremast climbing up the ratlines. Gordon Power and David Stevens ascend the mainmast. They practically vanish away up there. The fore gaff, which looks so small from the deck, is a big spar for Rick to straddle. The fore gaff topsail is the smallest sail on the ship — but at 580 square feet it is bigger than the entire sail plan of my 33-foot schooner.

The jib topsail goes rattling up its stay, its sheet running back almost to the wheel. The two gaff topsails take longer. Some of the lines are not properly led, and it takes a lot of calling back between the deck and the mastheads to get them hauled up the topmasts and out along the gaffs. The four masthead men are up there a long time.

"You know what the motion is like on deck," says Delbé Comeau. "Can you imagine what it's like aloft, even in calm weather? The first time you go up there, you're good for nothing except to hang on. You're absolutely terrified."

We all gaze up at Ian Morrison, nestled in the crosstrees, hanging on for dear life.

"You must have your heart in your mouth every time a new hand goes aloft," I remark.

"You do," nods Barr, shading his eyes. "But we've never had a man fall. They're so scared they just get super-careful. We had one fellow that was so scared we just had to let him go. He couldn't even go out on the bowsprit."

"The first time I was aloft, I was too scared even to be sick," smiles Delbé. "I was up there with Keith McLaren, the photographer. Keith was an old hand but I was just hanging on, and then Keith handed me the end of a line and said, 'Here, hold this', and he walked to the end of the spreaders and threw up, away out over the side. You're not over the deck up there, you know; on the lee side you're over the water.

"The motion up there is much worse than on a square-rigger. I made a trip on *Gazela Primiero*, the training ship they have in Philadelphia, taking her up to Maine for the winter. When we came out of the Cape Cod Canal on the Mass. Bay side, it was blowing a gale, and I had to go up and help take in a topgallant. Well, the motion up there in a full gale wasn't as bad as what it would be on this ship today."

"Feel her pick up speed?" Barr interjects. "Those tops'ls are so high they're getting more wind, and cleaner wind, less turbulence, than we're getting here on the deck. You can really feel her go. She's doing about nine knots right now, and the engines are off."

He's right. The big schooner is loping right along and there's hardly any wind.

"At this rate of going, we're going to have to slow her down," Barr says. "We're going to be there maybe thirty-six hours early, at this rate."

"Maybe we could duck into Cape May or some place," says Delbé. "We could use a day at anchor."

"Not many places to go on the Jersey coast," Barr answers. "Cape May's sixty miles from Atlantic City. We'd have to leave there first thing Saturday morning to make Atlantic City by noon."

Seventy feet overhead, Rick Moore is climbing around the forepeak halyards like a spider on a web. I'm reminded of Lloyd Heisler's favourite story about Angus Walters. In 1928 Heisler was a boy making his first fishing trip aboard *Bluenose*. He had grown up on Rous' Island, one of the dozens of small islands in Mahone Bay, and during a run from Lunenburg to Halifax in the fog, Walters sent him aloft to see what landmarks might be visible.

"I saw the Feather Lighthouse on Pearl Island," Heisler recalls. "I knew the Feather right well, I'd been out there lots of times with my father, so I sung out and told him 'Aaah, the Feather,' he said. 'You don't see the Feather, you see your old man's dung heap.' Well, good enough. I know what I seen, but I came back on deck.

"After a while, the skipper goes up aloft himself. By now we were pretty close to the island, headin' right for it. He didn't have the binoculars to his eyes too long before he called out, 'Haul her off! Haul her off!' When he got down on deck, I said, 'What's the matter, old man? Smell the shit?' He didn't say a thing — just spun around and walked away. But then he turned and he had a big grin on his face. After that we got along pretty good."

The authoritative Howard Chapelle contends that the racing schooners in particular were an aberration, a late and mutant flowering of a tradition that was essentially outdated when they were conceived. The racer, says Chapelle, was "no more than a special and technically minor adaptation.... She had no relation to fishing-schooner design, either as a descendant or as a parent," and she was generally "an economic failure."

The situation is not quite that clear. *Bluenose* paid her owners good dividends until the Depression blighted the entire fishery. Schooners had been stripped, tuned, and raced long before *Bluenose* was launched, and the *Dorothy M. Smart* was built with an eye to beating the *Albert J. Lutz* at least a decade earlier.

The difference between the International races and the innumerable formal and informal "hooks" among fishing schooners lay in the rivalry between Lunenburg and Gloucester, between Canadians and Americans, and even perhaps between "democrats" and "monarchists", or "revolutionaries" and "Loyalists." Many a speech writer has paid tribute to the profound kinship between Americans and Canadians, and only a fool would disregard the respect and affection the two peoples have repeatedly shown for one another, from the trenches of Europe and the embassy at Tehran to the hockey rinks and baseball fields. But for all this cordiality there are deep antagonisms, of which Canadians are inevitably more conscious than Americans. The United States is a highly ideological nation, one of the great powers of world history, with a sweeping sense of its own mission. Canada, by contrast, was assembled at a remnant sale when the financially troubled British Empire was selling off its inventory. We have always been an undernourished, inconspicuous cadet branch of the English-speaking family, living right next door to the imperial heir. We are a more cautious, more homogeneous, less venturesome people than the Americans. F. W. Wallace, himself a Canadian, points out that even in the schooner fishery it was the Americans, not the Canadians, who exploited the distant fishing grounds of Iceland, Greenland, and Africa. Canadians do not think of themselves as naturally victorious and we have no political and social theory to prove.

The Americans do have such theories, and they seek confirmation of them in the entrails of the most unlikely events. Thus the governor of Massachusetts, after *Esperanto*'s success in 1920, proclaimed that "the victory was a triumph for Americanism." It is hard to imagine a Canadian politician even thinking such a thing, let alone being silly enough to voice it; nor, one imagines, would the governor himself accept such views in reverse. Did *Bluenose*'s subsequent triumphs constitute "the defeat of Americanism?" And the governor was not some marginal eccentric given to fervid rhetoric; he was "Silent Cal" Coolidge, president of the United States.

After the 1938 series, Pine and Moulton complained bitterly that *Bluenose* had won her three races "in weather I don't consider fit for a fisherman's race," as Pine put it. "You could have paddled a canoe around the course the three days *Bluenose* won." Moulton peremptorily challenged Walters to race off Massachusetts for a five-hundred-dollar purse in winds of twenty-five knots or more. Walters huffily countered with a challenge to race either from Halifax or Boston to Bermuda and back to the other city, for a prize of five thousand dollars. Moulton said that was not enough money. Walters boosted it to twenty thousand dollars. No more was heard about the idea.

At the celebratory banquet, Walters was told that the three thousand dollars in prize money was not available and that the trophy had disappeared. He ordered *Bluenose* back to Nova Scotia at once — before she disappeared, too. The trophy turned up a day or so later on the front steps of an orphanage called the New England Home for Little Wanderers, with a verse attached:

Here's to Angus, good old sport,
Whose challenge sort of takes us short.
Give us a gale that blows at thirty
And we'll bet our shirts on little Gerty.

The eight thousand dollars offered by the New Englanders to help prepare *Bluenose* for racing was not paid either. Half was to have been advanced while *Bluenose* was in Lunenburg. It was not, and when Walters objected in Gloucester, he was given two thousand dollars. He wrote letters all winter, engaged a lawyer, and finally recovered forty-three hundred dollars.

None of this shows up in American accounts of the races, which one reads with rising amazement and indignation. Howard Chapelle was a devoted and tireless scholar whose work has enriched everyone who cares about sailing vessels. Yet even Chapelle declares that "there is no purpose to be served by recounting the history of each of the races, but all of those in which the Canadian Captain Walters sailed were distinguished by a complete lack of sportsmanship and by much bickering."

This is the same Angus Walters who doused his sails when *Ford* and *Elsie* lost their topmasts, who demanded that the race he lost to *Ford* be credited to his opponent, who registered no protest when Ben Pine made him choose collision or shipwreck on Sambro Ledges, who offered the only compromise over the series with *Columbia*. Certainly he could be a difficult man, proud, impetuous, domineering, and fiercely competitive. But he did not expect cheap or easy victories, and he had no use for men who knuckled under to him. He and his rigger, Paul Myra, made the waterfront tremble with the violence of their arguments; Myra would pull off his belt and snatch out his false teeth, setting them on a nearby piling, ready for a fistfight which never happened. But Walters respected Myra, as he respected Lloyd Heisler, for standing up to him. He told Lawrence Allen, his mate and friend, that their friendship could not have existed had Allen been afraid to speak his mind and stick to it.

And he was, as Chapelle puts it, "a prime sailor." Several other schooners might conceivably have been a match for *Bluenose* herself — *Puritan, Mayflower, Haligonian, Columbia* — but *Bluenose* was blessed with a master who knew her inside out, who fished her every season, who tuned her and steered her day after day, month after month, year after year. On the way to Gloucester in 1938, Walters brushed off everyone who came to speak to him. "The old girl's talkin' to herself," he would say. "I gotta listen to what she's sayin'." On the Banks, he would experiment with different ways to load her catch, different settings of the sails. During races, he would leave the wheel and go forward on deck, feeling her movements, looking, listening. Then he would hold up one finger, or two, and the helmsman would give her one or two more spokes of the wheel. He used his crew as movable ballast, sending them up forward or bringing them back aft until he was completely satisfied with the vessel's trim.

"He used to tune her for two weeks before a race," recalls Morris Allen — "Rigger Morris," as he is known in Lunenburg. "Change the ballast a little, recut a sail, take her out again. He wouldn't leave until she was just right. If someone had done all that with *Haligonian*, I think she could have beat *Bluenose*. I was fishing on *Haligonian* one time and we came up on *Bluenose*, got into a little hook there, and by God we did beat her." Randolph Stevens, David's great-grandfather, agreed. He was *Haligonian*'s sail trimmer when she beat *Bluenose* again at a Lunenburg fishermen's picnic in 1930, just before *Bluenose* lost the Lipton series.

None of this detracts from the vessel herself. But she could hardly have had such prolonged success without that intelligent, restless, persevering little skipper. When he lost a race, Angus Walters swallowed hard, congratulated the winner, reconsidered his strategy, and generally won the series. He had his faults, and all Lunenburg knew them, but he deserves the place he holds in the affections of Canadians as one of our few true national heroes.

And, for that matter, what was the "international" aspect of the whole thing all about? Almost all the masters Walters beat for the trophy — Ben Pine, Marty Welch, Clayton Morrissey — were "whitewashed Yankees," Nova Scotians, or Newfoundlanders who had moved to the States in search of opportunities they could not find at home. Fully half the Gloucester fleet was manned by Nova Scotians. At the end of *Fast and Able: Life Stories of Great Gloucester Fishing Vessels*, Gordon Thomas provides photos and short biographies of twelve of the greatest Gloucester captains: ten of them are Canadians, including Thomas's own father and uncle, natives of Arichat, Nova Scotia. When *Columbia* was lost in 1927, fourteen of her twenty-two drowned crewmen were Nova Scotians, including her master. The Gloucester crews were just about as "American" as a CFL football team is "Canadian."

Fundamentally, the races were competitions *within* a culture, not *between* cultures, and the legalism, jingoism, and general biliousness which at times overwhelmed the ships and their men are deeply disturbing because they represent a shallow falsehood overlaid on what was true, gracious, and invigorating. As Wendell Bradley points out, the sailors and shipwrights of the world share a multinational culture within which qualified people have always moved easily. A man who can sail a sampan or a dhow will find no lasting mystery in a schooner. The bickering and bitterness flowed not from the skippers and their crews, but from their backers and supporters, from writers, politicians, publicists, investors, and gamblers. Again and again, the committees and officials distorted what the skippers had understood to be fair and proper contests between the schooners: one partisan incorporated the violence of his opinions about the races into a successful campaign to become mayor of Gloucester. But Ben Pine and Angus Walters remained friends to the end of their lives, visiting back and forth at every opportunity.

What the races proved, if they really proved anything, was not the superiority of the American Way of Life, or the virtue of Lunenburg's dour conservatism. They proved simply that the east coast of North America could provide many fine designers, shipwrights, skippers, and sailors; they reminded us all — or should have — that there were many brave and capable men out fishing.

They are still there, too, in Lunenburg and Gloucester, men who routinely face the furies of the North Atlantic in order to bring the rest of us our supper.

After he sold *Bluenose*, Angus Walters was a haunted man. After she hit the reef, he even considered putting together an expedition to raise her. Once he knew she was irrevocably broken and gone, he began talking about building a replica — the only proper memorial to the great love of his life. He was an old man, and people took it to be no more than an old man's wistfulness.

But then, in the late 1950s, the Oland family, brewers of a beer called Schooner, began toying with the idea of building a schooner to promote the beer, or possibly a couple of small schooners to freight it. Then, in 1960, Metro-Goldwyn-Mayer needed a replica of Captain Bligh's *Bounty* and chose Smith and Rhuland to build her. Ellsworth Coggins was chosen to command her. He hired a crew of young Nova Scotians and sailed the replica to Tahiti for the shooting of *Mutiny on the Bounty*. Then he took her up and down both coasts of North America and over to Europe to promote the film.

Tourists had poured into Lunenburg to see *Bounty* being built. The ship had brought the town to the attention of the world. Angus Walters began to seem more like a visionary than a tottering old fool. If Lunenburg could build another *Bounty*, why not another *Bluenose*?

Walters and Lawrence Allen headed a committee to look into it. A replica would cost a quarter of a million dollars, and they hired a fund-raising consultant to examine the prospects of raising that much. The consultants reported that it could be done only with the support of a major corporation. The Olands had put their own plans aside, though they had agreed to purchase the *Bluenose* plans from Roue. They now met with Angus Walters. The Olands agreed to build and operate a replica, bringing her to Lunenburg every year for the fall Fisheries Exhibition and donating the profits from that week's activities to the exhibition. The new ship would be built at Smith and Rhuland and would spend as much time as possible in her home port. She would never be raced, lest she tarnish the name of *Bluenose*. And she would not freight beer.

Her name was to be *Bluenose II* — but that name had been reserved by Lawrence Allen, who was building a thirty-six-foot schooner for his own use. Lawrence Allen had been mate and master on *Gilbert B. Walters* and on a number of *Bluenose*'s later voyages — he brought her home from Gloucester in 1938 while Walters flew to meet his fiancée — and he describes Walters as "my best friend till the day he died." One day in 1963, Angus came to call on him.

"I got something to ask you, and it's a pretty big thing," said Angus. "If we can build a replica of the *Bluenose*, will you give up the name *Bluenose II*?"

"It is a big thing," said Allen. "Is it for yourself you're asking?"

"Yes," said Angus. "Will you do it for me?"

"I'll tell you what I'll do," said Allen. "The day the keel is laid for the new vessel, I'll give up the name."

The keel was laid February 27, 1963. Colonel Sidney Oland tapped the ceremonial spike. So did Bill Roue. Angus Walters drove it home. Lawrence Allen launched his own schooner just a week before *Bluenose II* slid down the ways that July. He called his little ship *Bluenose Jr.*

Twenty years later, *Bluenose II* is swinging along under everything but her fisherman's staysail, the huge quadrilateral that in light weather can be stretched between her mastheads.

"Trade wind weather," says Don Barr. "If we were in the trades, it would be just like this except the water would be twenty degrees warmer and the swells would be hundreds of feet apart."

"Sunfish!" comes a cry from the masthead. Everyone rushes to the starboard rail where a flat greenish-white disk wallows like a dead thing on the surface, falling rapidly astern. Ron Ottens, the engineer, has joined us — a big, round man originally from Massachusetts, now settled in Lunenburg. This is his first trip aboard.

"I almost feel guilty," says Ron, looking around the deck at the crewmen scraping, polishing, painting, seizing lines. "All this activity, and I got nothing to do." He's surprised at how fast she moves under sail, and for that matter, under power. The two 160-horsepower turbocharged Caterpillar diesels are not big engines for a ship of this size. The two diesel-powered generators, in fact, are not very much smaller.

"But the generators are far too big," Ron says. "They were put in when she was first built, when she had air conditioning for chartering down south in the winter, and that takes a lot of power. You look at the temperature gauge on that generator down below now. It doesn't even warm up. There's just no load on that generator."

A huge plane, eight jet engines streaming their contrails, dips down towards us, banks away, and arrows towards the horizon.

"B-52," says Ron, shading his eyes. He is a Vietnam veteran and an airplane buff. "Don't often see 'em that low." He laughs. "You can bet we're already being tracked by the Strategic Air Command."

Don and Delbé have been talking, and now they call our attention to a disturbance in the water a hundred yards to port.

"It looks like a tide rip," said Delbé.

"The edge of the Gulf Stream?" someone asks.

"No," says Don. "When you sail over the edge of the Gulf Stream, it's like sailing over a line drawn in the ocean. Right away the water is far warmer, and a different colour. There's no mistaking it."

"I wonder if there's a big change in the depth of water there."

Someone fetches the chart. Sure enough, we are sailing right along the edge of the Continental Shelf, where the water plunges from sixty fathoms to six hundred fathoms in a vertiginous sunken cliff face. Ocean currents press in on the land, shooting water up that cliff face, producing the froth and swirls we're seeing here on the surface. These waters are so easy, so seductive, that it is hard to realize that they could become the cauldron in which the ship met her first test, the hurricane of 1964.

Even without the hurricane, the maiden voyage of *Bluenose II* was a thoroughly romantic adventure. She was sailing to the Pacific under Ellsworth Coggins to search for treasure on Cocos Island. Three hundred miles off the coast of Panama, Cocos is believed to have been the base of a pirate named Benito Benito, who in the 1820s stripped the treasures from many Peruvian churches. The expedition yielded a film by Taylor Television entitled *Expedition Bluenose* but recovered no treasure.

Capt. Coggins is a plump, cheerful little man who is ostensibly retired, living in a trim bungalow set among spacious gardens in the rolling green farmland of the Annapolis Valley. He shipped out on a schooner for twelve dollars a month when he was sixteen, and two years later, by a series of accidents, found himself in command.

While his wife Pauline hulls a large bowl of strawberries and occasionally corrects his memory of facts and dates, Coggins, now sixty-nine, talks about the voyages he still makes from time to time — he is just back from two trips to the southern United States as relief mate aboard gypsum boats from nearby Hantsport — and remembers his years as the first master of *Bluenose II.*

Colonel Sidney Oland had three sons, Victor, Bruce, and Don, and though Don did most of the actual management of the ship, the colonel was the ultimate authority, a point Coggins insisted on clarifying at the outset. During the summer the ship offered harbour tours in Halifax, but also travelled the Maritimes, visiting local events such as the lobster carnivals in Shediac and Pictou, Old Home Week in Charlottetown, and the Festival of the Strait at Port Hawkesbury. She generally made a trip up the Bay of Fundy to Digby and Saint John, and she invariably attended the Fisheries Exhibition in Lunenburg.

In December or January she went south, carrying charter parties in the West Indies. "We had no set port we were based in," Coggins says. "In fact we got into the charter business by accident. The first winter we were down there, the colonel was going to come down with a party of guests for a couple of weeks, and then each of the sons was going to do the same and that way we'd pretty well use up the winter. But then friends of the Olands' friends wanted to know if they couldn't get a trip on her, too, and before we knew it we were booked up for the whole winter. We'd pick up a group in Grenada, say, and take them up the islands to Antigua, then pick up another group there and take them somewhere else."

The crew consisted of master, mate, chief engineer, cook, steward, bosun, and seven deckhands. George Snow, the bosun, had been Coggins's bosun on *Bounty*, and had also sailed as seaman and mate on the first *Bluenose*. The crew worked year-round, with a month's leave when the ship was laid up for spring refit. Most stayed a year or two, but some stayed much longer. Oddmund Skoje, who was to succeed Coggins as master, served six years as mate. To some extent, the ship paid her own way through harbour tours and charter fees, but Oland subsidized her substantially — some reports say to the tune of $100,000 a year. As Coggins points out, however, "That's not very much in an advertising budget. How many full-page ads in magazines could you get for that?"

In 1967, following *Bluenose*'s precedent, *Bluenose II* made her way up the St. Lawrence to Montreal, where she acted as host ship at Expo. Dignitaries arriving by water were berthed behind her and welcomed at receptions aboard the schooner. At other times, she was open to visitors at the fair. Concerned about her exposure to fresh water, which breeds rot, Coggins and his crew kept her structure "pickled" by pouring 350 pounds a week of rock salt into her bilges. Coggins, who is a gregarious and companionable man, enjoyed the time at Expo and happily recalls entertaining such dignitaries as Robert Stanfield, who was then running for the federal Tory leadership. The extent of the entertainment may be judged by the liquor bill which hovered around $1,200 a week. In 1967, that meant much merriment.

By the end of the season, visitors had worn down the hard-pine and Douglas fir decks so badly that they had to be planed and sanded down a full half-inch to bring them true again. Meanwhile, on the fairgrounds themselves, David Stevens's father and grandfather were delighting thousands of visitors by building a wooden schooner right in the Atlantic Provinces Pavilion. Her name was *Atlantica* and she is still going strong. Her prototype, *Avenger*, now belongs to the playwright and folk singer Tom Gallant, and while we sailed *Bluenose II* south in the spring of 1983, *Avenger* was sailing north, back to Nova Scotia after a winter in the Lesser Antilles.

Ellsworth Coggins commanded *Bluenose II* longer than any other single master and he retains a marked fondness for her. He regards Don Barr, for example, with something of the attitude one might take towards the spouse of a childhood sweetheart. He wonders why Barr has never taken his sailing master's ticket, and he disapproves of Barr's habit of leaving the jib gaskets hanging loose. Coggins always triced them up neatly over the bowsprit. He talks with pride about his changes to the rigging — adding double topping lifts and lazy jacks, and, after cracking the mainmast one time, adding an extra shroud and lengthening the chain-plates by eighteen inches. Her original sails were #0 canvas. The mainsail weighed 1500 pounds dry and twice that much wet. Furling it was like trying to fold plywood, and a suit of sails lasted three years. Coggins oversaw the change to Dacron, which he considers a vast improvement.

"All the old skippers in Lunenburg said I carried too much sail," he smiles. "Angus Walters said that himself. I used to carry topsails in fifty-five knots. She was fast. We left Halifax once with the storm trysail instead of the main and changed over after we crossed the Gulf Stream. On that trip we made eighteen hundred miles in seven days, Halifax to San Juan, Puerto Rico. We were on the same tack all the way down. Another time I remember going from Halifax to Lunenburg, with all sail set and no wind to speak of, not a ripple of the water, and she was still ghosting along at five knots.

"We used to take a crew of cadets from Sydney to St. Pierre or Corner Brook every fall, just three regular crew and fifteen cadets. One year it was blowing hard, forty or forty-five knots, and I only hoisted the jumbo. She averaged nine knots all the way down to St. Pierre under just the jumbo. She'd make twelve or fourteen knots so easy, with so small a breeze you wouldn't believe it. Officially, she never raced, you know, but unofficially we never let anything pass us."

The fastest he ever saw her travel was on the way north from the Caribbean in 1968. At four o'clock in the morning, sailing uneventfully under her five lower sails, *Bluenose II* was caught in a small tornado.

"I saw the wind gauge go up over one hundred miles per hour and after that I was too busy to look again," Coggins remembers. "We ran off before it, and she was being driven so hard her bow went away down, and there were gushers of water driving in on deck through the hawse-holes. In the days of sail, there were ships sailed right under, and that's just what it was like. She must have been doing twenty-one or twenty-two knots until the mainsail split. It split right from boom to gaff. The tornado didn't last very long, but I think she was on the verge of running under."

By the end of the 1960s, *Bluenose II* was in need of work. Her stern had already been rebuilt when she was only three years old. Because she carries passengers, she falls under Canada's steamship inspections, which require a watertight bulkhead just abaft her cabin. But the regulations were designed for steel motor ships, not for wooden schooners, and the lack of ventilation has made the stern a fertile breeding ground for rot. It has since been replaced again at least twice, most recently in 1983.

The rot was not confined to the stern. Sealed up by panelling below, her accommodations kept cool by air conditioning while the tropic sun beat on her decks and topsides *Bluenose II* had been troubled with condensation, which produces rot. Meanwhile, the Olands were negotiating to sell their brewery to John Labatt, Ltd., and as they had no further use for the ship, they laid off the crew and tied her up. She might have fetched $750,000 on the market, rot and all. But how could they sell Nova Scotia's symbolic ship, particularly to a buyer anywhere else?

"Can you imagine what would have happened if we'd done that?" asks Bruce Oland. "Our family would have been drummed out of the province. *Those are the men that sold the Bluenose.* We couldn't have walked down a street in Halifax. We realized right from the beginning that although we might be doing the work and paying the bills, the ship belonged to the people of Nova Scotia."

In September 1971 the Olands sold *Bluenose II* to the government of Nova Scotia for a dollar. The ship was tied to a Halifax pier without a crew, stripped of her certificate of seaworthiness. The air was filled with cries of "ripoff!" and "bail out!" The minister of tourism, Garnet Brown, objected. It was, he said, a fine, generous gesture by a great Nova Scotia family firm. Dartmouth broadcaster Arnie Patterson headed up a fund-raising committee to pay for the refit, which the province could not afford. He did an amazing job. All across Canada, schoolchildren sent in "Bluenose dimes," while Patterson and his committee canvassed private and corporate donors. The Olands themselves kicked off the drive with a contribution of $50,000. In the end, the 1972-73 refit cost $250,000, and of this, $155,000 came from the people of Nova Scotia and Canada.

By 1973 *Bluenose II* was taking harbour tours under Oddmund Skoje. In 1974, as high oil prices strangled American consumers, tourism minister Glen Bagnell announced that *Bluenose II* would make a promotional tour of the U.S. east coast, visiting Norfolk, Washington, Annapolis, Baltimore, Philadelphia, New York, New Haven, New Bedford, Boston, Gloucester, Portland, and Bar Harbour. It was fitting, said Bagnell smugly, that in view of the fuel shortage, Nova Scotia should make "an official visit to our good friends in the United States by way of a sailing vessel," and he assured tourists that there would be ample gasoline in Nova Scotia that summer. "From New England, at least, a tankful of gasoline will get you to our province, and we will have enough fuel to make sure you get home as well."

Alas, the tour was a comedy of errors — a fit beginning to the Gilbert and Sullivan phase of the ship's life. As columnist Harry Bruce put it, she became "joke-fated," Nova Scotia's "beloved bungler of the bounding main."

In Norfolk she cracked her bowsprit on a bundle of pilings while berthing. In Gloucester she was greeted with a scornful cutline in the *Daily Times:* "*Bluenose II* enters the harbour yesterday 'under full diesel.'" Skoje, a native of Norway who had spent most of his life on motor vessels, was exceptionally cautious about sailing — which may have been prudent but was far from dashing. Skoje was also a shy man, desperately uncomfortable at receptions and parties.

At the end of the season, Skoje was dismissed over what were described as disagreements over the promotional role of the captain. Despite the problems, the trip worked. An estimated fifty thousand Americans visited the vessel and more than two thousand travel-industry representatives were entertained aboard. Largely as a result of the trip, the number of U.S. tourists visiting Nova Scotia went up 18.5 percent over 1973 and the province won a Silver Anvil award from the Public Relations Society of America for what was considered an imaginative and successful promotion.

The following year, *Bluenose II* set off in April for a similar tour of fourteen ports in the Great Lakes. The new captain was Ernest Hartling, sixty-nine, a retired Halifax harbour pilot. He was a handsome and robust man who told reporters it was "a distinct honour to serve this beautiful lady as master." The new first mate was Fred Copas, a former skipper of the supply ship Cape Scott and a veteran of the Canadian navy. Just outside Halifax, *Bluenose II* struck gale-force winds and heavy seas which delayed her arrival in Montreal where she was to be fitted with a new sewage system. Since she had not been planned for holding tanks, the tanks had to be erected on deck.

Thus awkwardly equipped to enter the pristine waters of Lake Ontario, she arrived in Rochester, New York, on May 18 with a deck cargo of fermenting sewage. There, she was boarded by three advertising executives named James Nelson, Christian Rugh, and Sharon Jenkins. This salty trio was appalled by the ship's condition and promptly fired off a letter to Glen Bagnell, thoughtfully releasing it first to the press. *Bluenose II*, they said, was "in terrible shape," with "great unpainted patches on her topsides and very tired varnish on her spars." The crew had no "identifying clothing" aside from one *Bluenose II* T-shirt and "some crew members were even wearing cowboy boots and several were sitting around the hatches, drinking beer and watching visitors. Empty cans and bottles were around the deck." There were no guides or literature and the U.S. courtesy flag was flying where the crew's meal flag properly belonged.

"Given command," they concluded, "in two weeks any one of us would have the boat gold plated and the crew either shaped up or shipped out."

Offering various explanations, Bagnell dismissed the letter as "a total pile of crap," a phrase that applied equally well to the Ontario sewage crisis which now burst upon him. An unnamed Ontario environment ministry official announced that unless *Bluenose II* met Ontario's sewage disposal requirements, she would be "drummed off the Great Lakes." As the schooner ambled along the U.S. shore from Rochester to Buffalo, Erie, Cleveland, Toledo, and Detroit, the mystery deepened. Why had Ontario not made a simple phone call to Halifax which would have revealed that the holding tanks were already in place? One Nova Scotian official said he was sure that *Bluenose II* would meet the requirements. Another invited Ontario's inspectors to "stick their heads in and have a real good look."

In Windsor, Ontario's inspectors approved the tanks and environment minister William Newman boarded the ship. He said the whole thing was "probably a misunderstanding. We knew as far back as January that everything was in order. There was never any doubt that the holding tanks would be approved." The *Windsor Star* registered the only judgment that made any sense of all this: It considered the whole affair to be promotion for Ontario's clean-water enforcement programme and chided Newman's department for "new lows in publicity grabbing."

After six weeks and four thousand miles, the schooner returned to a warm welcome in Halifax. In the distance however, one might have heard the chuckles of the gods. The libretto for the next year's comic triumph was already being written. The U.S. government had invited *Bluenose II* to participate in the Bicentennial Parade of Sail in New York. This provided the occasion for a long tour of the U.S. coast. And in Cleveland, Capt. Hartling had commenced a relationship with another "beautiful lady" — a forty-six-year-old widow with the improbable name of Mary Smith.

Friday — Graveyard Watch

I was on deck shortly before ten o'clock tonight, talking with Rick Moore and enjoying the evening. The moon hung low, huge and orange above the eastern horizon, its lower limb cut off by a charcoal bank of fog.

"Look at that moon," said Ian Morrison happily. "You know, it came up tonight just like it was coming out of an envelope."

"Rick," said Jeff Steeves, at the wheel, "the light's out in the compass."

Rick dropped below into the chart room, popped on deck again, and hurried forward to the engine room. The compass light turned out to be a symptom of real trouble in the electrical system. Now, at midnight, all the electronics are out — Loran, sat nav, radar, echo sounder, direction finder, everything. The batteries are dead. The engines can't be started. Ron is working steadily, has been for hours, will be for the rest of the night. He emerges occasionally from the engine room, sweaty and greasy, to smoke a cigarette or ask for someone to come hold a light. The engineer has no set watch. He is always on call. Ron wryly remembers his comment yesterday that he felt guilty with everyone else working. Tonight all three watches will come and go before he gets a chance to rest.

The fundamental problem is the new radar. The old one ran off the AC generator and gave a lot of trouble, so the new one runs off the batteries. Ron warned before we left that the batteries would handle the systems already on them, but couldn't provide enough power for the radar as well. The installers denied this. "When someone like that tells me I don't know my business," says Ron, "I do a slow fry." But we sailed without the extra converter Ron wanted to install, and events have proven him correct. This is no great consolation, eighty-five miles from New York and seventy miles south of Montauk.

So *Bluenose II* has suddenly become *Bluenose*, reliant on chart and compass, lead line and lookout. We are nearly back to 1920, though the generator is running and we do have electric lights. Delbé has asked for a lookout in the bow, and I am sitting astride the bowsprit, the red and green of the running lights in the foremast shrouds glowing softly on the furled jib in front of me, my back against the jumbo stay as it flexes and relaxes, flexes and relaxes. Twenty feet ahead, the tip of the bowsprit quests for the distant American coast like the nose of an eager hound. *Bluenose II* is sailing under her lowers only, restless as always. Off her port quarter, a nervous, silver moon path stirs on the ocean. Far on the port beam, a circular patch of sea gleams where the moonlight strikes down through a break in the distant clouds. The curved blade of the ship's stem lifts on a swell, then swings down through marbled foam.

Nothing ahead. I look astern along the white sweep of the rail cap stark in the moonlight, the wet decks, the lace of the rigging against the bright acreage of canvas. From the bow, the ship's body is narrow and elongated. (From aloft, Delbé says, she is "like a needle.") The wheel seems far away, with its cluster of dark human forms and the orange dot of Delbé's cigarette. The long dark swells rise up astern, lift the schooner, push her forward, raise the bows and drop them as they run ahead and leave her behind. The mastheads describe parabolas around a single zenith star.

A fragile, transient, mortal night.

I wish we were going further. Much, much further.

"A few days out here is worth a good many hours at the head shrinker," says Delbé.

"You can't stay on this thing very long without becoming religious," says David Stevens.

"I think I can," says Brian Steeves, his eyes fixed on the compass. As befits a modern student of philosophy, he is a devout materialist, a human sacrifice on the altar of logical positivism.

Everyone sighs with pleasure. Here is a topic of no practical urgency, big enough to occupy all the rest of the watch and promising more happy hours of warm and inconclusive debate through the whole duration of the voyage. It is the perfect topic for a night like this, when it is easy to imagine God Himself listening in with amusement and being tempted to express an opinion from time to time.

Sailing is not so much a job as a calling, a vocation. Voyaging is one of the great metaphors for life itself — life stripped of its fever and fret, focussed on ultimate concerns. The mysterious, tragic quality of the sea echoes the unknowable reaches of the human situation, of our relation to chance and destiny, glory and disaster. Sailing requires a powerful development of crucial human qualities: courage, determination, ingenuity, cooperation, honesty, competence. The sailor daily confronts the possibility of suffering and privation, even of death. Like one or two other ventures — mining and battle, for instance — sailing makes great demands on people and bonds them closely together in the full recognition of their interdependence despite their human frailty. It is understandable, as Noel Mostert puts it, that "for so many centuries shipwreck struck man as the epitome of irony and despair: the failure of himself at his proven best, within a rope's throw of salvation."

Because his life is founded on risk, the seaman develops attitudes alien to the landsman. Deference, humility, subordination of his own needs to those of the ship — these develop organically, the natural outgrowth of increased understanding. A profound conservatism marks the nautical character, a realization that innovations and bright ideas which work well on the dry and stable foundation of the land may well fail when plunged repeatedly into salt water, buffeted by gales, smashed by expectable accidents. The cost of their failure will not be reckoned in cash or inconvenience but in lives. *Bluenose II* carries modern electronics, but it would be unthinkable to throw away the sextant, the magnetic compass, the chart, and the lead line on the assumption that the electronics will always work. There are old sailors, runs a famous adage, and there are bold sailors, but there are no old, bold sailors.

These habits of mind are really matters of faith — faith in one's own ability, in one's comrades, in the ship. Faith in technology, or in Providence. Superstition and religion are indeed parallel and logical responses to the marine experience. Notwithstanding its semiconductors, *Bluenose II* represents an anthology of ideas which have proven themselves for periods long enough to warrant the faith of seamen. "No designer or builder can have full experience in all things pertaining to vessels," writes the deeply traditional designer R. D. Culler, "but they can and should be very much guided by what worked in the past."

The role of chance, of the gods, is obvious in life at sea. Their role is equally large ashore, but it is easily overlooked amidst the clatter and roar of peripheral matters. Going to sea, in the New England phrase, "centres a man down", and puts his life's concerns into perspective. "Do you realize," said Ian Morrison suddenly this afternoon, "that we've heard nothing about the Tory leadership?" Everyone looked pleased at the thought. We sail beyond politics, in a sense, into a region where the soul naturally contemplates its origins and destiny. Hence the power of the voyaging metaphor, casting into sharp relief the essence of all our ventures.

No wonder then that the sea has contributed so much to our language — a language evolved by an island people and spread around the world by sea. No wonder, also, that a Pole setting out to become the greatest marine author in history, Joseph Conrad, should write in this foreign tongue, for English was the language of seafaring, so deeply marked by the sea that most of its native speakers would not even recognize such terms as *son of a gun, swing a cat, two shakes, bitter end, devil to pay, flogging a dead horse,* and *scuttlebutt* for what they are: nautical metaphors buried so deeply in the language that the language has forgotten they are metaphors.

The repetition and discipline of life aboard a ship breed traditions as naturally as a tree bears fruit. Brian and I, for example, always go below on the graveyard watch to raid the galley for hot chocolate, apples, and wieners, or "tube steaks", as Brian calls them. Why us? Why these refreshments? Why the same thing every watch?

No matter. Crunching apples, sipping hot chocolate, the watch settles into serious philosophical disputation. I take the wheel. Listening to their speculations, I realize that I have developed a powerful affection for the vessel and her style of life, and for my comrades, who are beginning to emerge for me as distinct and admirable human beings. In no other circumstance would we know one another so well or so quickly. David Stevens remarks that once this happens, one actually sleeps more soundly, certain that the ship and your own welfare are in capable hands. A new warmth shows in the jokes, which are based on personal foibles. Charlie, for instance, is becoming famous for burned toast. By the end of the summer, he will no doubt be known as "Cinders" or something of the kind. Last night, the boys were watching a movie on the videotape recorder in the salon and the image was almost obscured by dense clouds of smoke from the galley. No one stirred. They just yelled for Charlie who, sure enough, had forgotten he had put some toast on.

And the ship herself seems to have become animate, a loyal, intimate, trustworthy fellow adventurer.

"Good," says Delbé, when I mention this. "I thought you'd understand things like that if you could make the trip with us."

"I can understand how a person could forget that the ship belongs to the Nova Scotia government."

"Out here, she doesn't belong to them," says Delbé. "She belongs to us. All the government has to do with it is that they tell us which ports to visit."

At three a.m. we hear a whir and a roar, and Ron Ottens comes on deck looking happy. He has one engine going; he'll soon have the other one, too. He's apprehensive about Atlantic City. The entrance to the harbour is a narrow cut through a sandbar with a fierce tidal current, and Don Barr is anxious to have full power available if he needs it. He'll have it, says Ron, but we may have to run the engines continuous until we get there. He flips his cigarette into the blackness overside and goes below again.

The illusion that the ship belonged to him and not to the government is the way many people account for the behaviour of Capt. Hartling during the 1976 cruise to New Orleans. Don Barr was then second mate, and his crewmen from *Hilda Gerard*, Delbé Comeau and Richie LeBlanc, were able seamen. The voyage was one of the more outlandish episodes in the nautical history of Nova Scotia, the acme of the Gilbert and Sullivan period of *Bluenose II*.

It may be that Bomber Forbes established the basic tone of the voyage. Gerald Forbes was a legendary Halifax character, fifty-two years old in 1976 and known as "Bomber" for his heavy hitting as a youthful softball player. During the 1960s, Forbes operated the Shipbuilders Club, owned by the Halifax dockyard unions. Membership, however, was open to anyone, and there were few other places in Halifax to meet for a late-night drink. As a result, the club was much frequented by sportsmen, politicians, labour officials, and other night hawks.

By some labyrinthine political process, Bomber became cook on *Bluenose II*. He was not an exceptionally good choice. For one thing, he was a triumphantly grubby man, inhabiting the same T-shirt for weeks at a time and given to dishing out spaghetti with his bare hands. He was a chain smoker who coughed constantly. He kept an ice-cream scoop in a five-gallon pail of lard beside the stove. Even the breakfast bacon was fried in lard. "There was only one way to have eggs," smiles Delbé Comeau. "Poached. In lard." *Bluenose II* was a floating epidemic of burping and heartburn.

They left Halifax on April 15. The basic plan of the cruise was to sail to Mobile, Alabama, do some maintenance on the ship, and proceed to New Orleans. The ship would then return to New York for Operation Sail on July 4, with many stops at southern U.S. ports along the way. So *Bluenose II* arrived at Norfolk, Virginia, on April 21. She was not supposed to stop at Norfolk at all, though. She was supposed to stop at Morehead City, North Carolina, instead.

They left Norfolk on April 22, ostensibly for Mobile. Off the coast of Florida, however, Hartling came into the chart room, peered at the chart, and directed Don Barr to alter course to the westward. Barr knew that Hartling was shortsighted and assumed he'd misread the chart.

"If I alter here, sir," he said, "we'll run her ashore at Fort Lauderdale."

"Ah!" said Hartling. "You're getting the idea!"

Hartling had already made it clear to Barr that a second mate was a very low form of life. He was expected to appear for meals on time, listen to the conversation of the captain and the chief engineer, remain until he was instructed to leave, and speak only when spoken to. First mate Fred Copas was under similar restrictions, but when Copas wanted to leave he would invent an item of ship's business that required his attention and Hartling would excuse him. Barr tried this one time, claiming he had a crew of men scraping the bowsprit or some such thing, and that he should check their progress.

"You stay right where you are," Hartling said, smiling. "I know perfectly well that Copas has nothing to do either, but he's the first mate, so I let him leave. You're the second mate. You stay."

So Barr turned the ship west. *Bluenose II* arrived in Fort Lauderdale on April 27. Waiting on the wharf was Mary Smith from Cleveland. The captain, whose wife was at home in Dartmouth, welcomed her aboard, and they slipped their lines for Mobile the next afternoon.

The mere fact of a female guest was not in itself remarkable. Bomber Forbes had brought a girl friend by the name of Maxine MacDonald who was fully capable of keeping Bomber in line. At various points, the engineer's wife was aboard and so was Tricia Barr.

Mrs. Smith, however, was quite remarkable. She kept Bomber and his steward hustling for strawberry shortcake, ice for her whisky, and other niceties. She brought two of her seven children aboard, and one of her sons brought a buddy from the U.S. Air Force. The crew became restive.

They arrived in Mobile on May 2 and stayed ten days, sandblasting the hull, scraping, and painting. On May 12 they left. The next day a Mississippi River pilot ran them onto a mudbank. They got off under their own power and arrived in New Orleans that evening. Alas, they were not due until the next morning, when a gala arrival had been arranged by Nova Scotia's tourism department, complete with fireboats, a band on the wharf, and a civic welcome. One can imagine the consternation of the tourism officials when, that morning, they found *Bluenose II* already secured — to the wrong wharf — and the captain departed to a hotel with Mrs. Smith.

The next day saw a reception aboard the ship and in a building on the adjacent wharf. And here, apparently, Hartling made his grievous error. He introduced Mary Smith as the ship's purser. Newsmen were fascinated. An American widow, purser on *Bluenose II*? What an angle! The story went out on the wire service, and the wire service carried it to Nova Scotia, where it caused no little consternation. *Dear Mr. Premier: If* Bluenose II *is going to have a female purser, why not me? At least I'm a Nova Scotian....*

"That reference to Mary was the only down point in a really good reception," remembers Mike Patrick, then the marketing director for Nova Scotia's tourism department. "Ernie was a wonderful public speaker, much better than many of the politicians, and whenever he spoke he was always able to do a great job for U.S.-Canadian relations. He was just the kind of old sea dog people dream about meeting on a great sailing ship like that.

"By and large I got on really well with Ernie. He was a very gregarious man, always great fun. But I had to report what was going on, and Ernie certainly didn't like to be crossed."

On May 17, they left New Orleans, with Patrick aboard. Slicing along through the Gulf of Mexico, *Bluenose II* was in danger of arriving in Miami a full day early. To kill time, she stopped in the Dry Tortugas for a memorable day-long picnic. Mrs. Smith, however, was feeling more and more at home, almost as though the ship were her own yacht. And back home, the storm over her presence was rising.

In Miami, deputy minister of tourism Bill Ozard met the ship and ordered all the female guests to disembark. Hartling demurred. He was master of the ship and he would decide who should be aboard and who should not. The servants were civil. They would, if need be, hire a car for Mary Smith. She could drive from port to port. What Hartling did with his time ashore was his own business. But Mrs. Smith was not a part of the ship's complement, period.

Hartling reluctantly agreed. When *Bluenose II* sailed for Jacksonville on May 25, Mary Smith was *not* aboard, Bill Ozard was aboard, and Ernest Hartling was not happy.

Jacksonville, Jacksonville. So much happened in Jacksonville.

Smith and Hartling were reunited and took themselves off to a hotel. A delegation from the local yacht club appeared and invited the ship's officers to a little dinner at the club. Copas, Barr, and Ozard went along in Hartling's place. When they arrived, they found the club was housed in the oldest building in the United States, built in the sixteenth century by Ponce de Leon, and the "little dinner" was a large and formal affair with the cream of Jacksonville society. Libations were frequent and serious — cocktails before dinner, superb wines with the meal, several Rusty Nails afterwards — and when the hosts offered to show the *Bluenose II* men around the building, Fred Copas's knees were not equal to the task of supporting him. He fell backward, grabbed the table behind him, and upended it along with six or eight formally dressed couples and their meals. There were no further dinner invitations during the four days the ship lay in Jacksonville.

Delbé Comeau and Richie LeBlanc were faring better. Two young women had appeared to watch the ship's arrival. Richie needed an opportunity to hear the new record albums he had bought on the trip. The girls invited him to use their stereo. In response, the sailors offered to take the ladies for dinner. At about the time Copas was tumbling in the yacht club, Comeau was luxuriating by candlelight in a bubble bath. The smell of incense filled the air. He had a glass of wine in his hand, and a beautiful, friendly girl to scrub his back. We draw the curtain of modesty, gentle reader, over the balance of this and the two subsequent evenings in the lives of these jolly tars.

While the crew cavorted, Hartling snorted. Ozard and Patrick had flown home, leaving the ship to be managed by contract representatives. Just before the ship was to sail, a covey of reporters converged on the wharf. Hartling held a brief, impromptu press conference in front of the appalled tourism functionaries. He told the press that he was the captain of the ship and he was responsible for the people aboard her. His professional sphere of influence was being infringed upon by office-bound dingbats who knew nothing of nautical responsibilities. They had removed Mary Smith. He was going to take Mary Smith back on board and if the fancy hats from Halifax wanted to do anything about it, they could do it in their fancy hats. Or words to that effect.

Bluenose II sailed away with Mary Smith aboard. The tourism representatives gazed at the schooner's defiant transom in disbelief.

Diplomatic relations between Halifax and *Bluenose II* came to an abrupt and ominous halt. When the ship arrived in Savannah, Georgia, the next day, there was no one from Nova Scotia waiting on the wharf, no civic reception laid on, no visit from the Canadian consul. But Comeau and LeBlanc were entranced to see a car they knew. The ladies from Jacksonville had driven up to meet them.

There were no officials in Charleston, South Carolina, and this time there were no ladies, either. Regretfully, Delbé sent a tender message and six red roses by wire to Jacksonville — one for each magic night — and *Bluenose II* sailed for Norfolk.

There was no reception party in Norfolk, either. There was none in Portsmouth or Newport News or Fort Eustis.

In Washington, Prime Minister Trudeau was expected aboard. Uncharacteristically, Hartling took *Bluenose II* in under sail. The berth to which she had been directed was a long finger pier at Washington Marina. Men were stationed at the sheets, ready to let the sails fly broad off as the ship came alongside. Others were detailed to jump onto the wharf, surge the dock lines around the bollards, and stop the ship. As the schooner came closer, the crew could see the reception party: civic officials, TV cameras on tripods, a band.

Bluenose II slid up to her berth. The sails were let fly. But something went wrong. The wind was by now astern, and letting the sails fly simply gave them more wind and gave the ship more speed. The booms swung out over the floating pier about three feet above the deck and moving fast.

The reception party faced two enormous spars sweeping inexorably down the wharf. People flopped on their faces. Cameras were knocked over. Musicians scrambled for safety. People jumped into the water.

The crewmen scrambled onto the wharf with the mooring lines. There were no bollards, only small cleats, nothing big enough to hold *Bluenose II*'s lines. There was no way to stop her at all. Her 285 tons moved relentlessly along the wharf and up onto the beach, poking the bowsprit through a section of brand-new chain-link fence. Hartling ordered the engines reversed. She had grounded gently and she backed off without difficulty.

So did the chain-link fence, clinging to the bowsprit like a Chinese finger puzzle.

Pierre Elliott Trudeau came aboard forty-five minutes later. The logbook does not record his comments, if he made any. He left after fifteen minutes.

There were no tourism officers to greet the ship at the U.S. Naval Academy in Annapolis when she arrived on June 19. There were none in Baltimore on June 22. When Mike Patrick met the ship in Philadelphia on June 24, Mary Smith was still aboard and the crew was mutinous.

Delbé Comeau went ashore in Philadelphia and phoned the lady in Jacksonville. He was electrified to learn that she had received the roses, resigned her job, loaded her car, and departed for Nova Scotia. She would meet him in New

York, which she did. The two subsequently spent six months together in Nova Scotia.

On June 29, *Bluenose II* was scheduled to slip her lines at two o'clock and depart from Philadelphia. She was lying in a small artificial basin with big, new, shiny aluminum guardrails all around it. At one o'clock Don Barr was on deck. He looked up to see four men walking down the wharf. One was the Canadian consul in Philadelphia. Another was Bill Ozard. The third was Mike Patrick. The fourth was Capt. Andrew C. Thomas. They came aboard and asked for the captain. Barr said the captain was below. Ozard went below to see Hartling in his quarters.

A moment later, Mary Smith came on deck. She was crying, and looking for Bomber Forbes. Soon after, Ozard and Hartling came up the companionway. Ozard introduced Hartling to Thomas.

"Captain Hartling," said Ozard, "Captain Thomas will be replacing you in command of this ship, effective immediately." He looked at his watch. "She is due to leave for New York in one hour and we want her to leave on time."

Hartling left with Mary Smith, but their epilogue makes the whole affair something finer than an old sea dog's casual amour. They were genuinely in love, and they are now married and living happily ever after in Ohio and Florida.

Bomber Forbes, a man of principle, resigned in protest.

Capt. Thomas is the first to admit he knew nothing about sailing vessels. His command began inauspiciously. The ship did leave on time, but before she could get out of the boat basin she had to be turned end for end, moving forward and back in roughly the way a car is moved out of a tight parallel-parking spot. The task was almost impossible, and Thomas had never been aboard the vessel before that moment. Every time she went forward, her bowsprit demolished one of the aluminum guardrails in front of her. Every time she went astern, her projecting main boom threatened another one. A harbour tug was enlisted. By the time she departed, *Bluenose II* had made a remarkably clean sweep of the shiny new rails.

She sailed on down Chesapeake Bay and up the coast to Sandy Hook off New York. On July 4, along with fifteen square-riggers from fourteen nations and innumerable smaller vessels such as *Bluenose II* herself, she sailed up the Hudson River. Buildings along the shore were jammed with people. Light planes and helicopters hurried overhead. The river was clogged with spectator boats packed solid along the lane up which the Operation Sail parade moved. *Bluenose II* was the largest, and the first, of the Class B ships, and the spectator boats took advantage of the gap between her and the Class A square-riggers to cut back and forth from one side to the other. A U.S. Coast Guard officer was aboard *Bluenose II* and a small cutter escorted her. As the cutter cleared her path ahead, *Bluenose II*'s crew were horrified to see a small power cruiser anchored fifty feet dead ahead. The schooner cannot even begin to stop in fifty feet. If she swerved to either side, she would demolish six or eight spectator boats.

"Hold your course, sir," said the Coast Guard officer.

The owner of the cruiser — whose engine had failed and left him in this dire predicament — saw the curving bow coming at him and began frantically pulling in his anchor line. This action probably saved his life, because it pulled him slightly off the ship's direct path. But *Bluenose II* had her anchors hanging off their catheads at either side, ready to be let go instantly if needed. Her port anchor hooked the little cruiser just below the deck line. It ripped her cabin right off. The wreck bumped and scraped along the full length of the larger ship without her deck beams to stiffen her. When Don Barr looked astern, the cutter was pulling the couple out of the water and, "I don't think there was one square yard of hull or deck left in one piece."

On July 10, at two o'clock in the afternoon, *Bluenose II* tied up at Privateer's Wharf in Halifax. It had been quite a cruise.

Capt. Thomas's home is in Indian Point, almost next door to Don Barr's. The roomy, comfortable house is surrounded by the kinds of gardens and shrubs that take decades to develop. A wide verandah opens a prospect through the trees to the shores and waterways of island-speckled Mahone Bay. Andrew Thomas was raised here, and so were his children. A plastic sign is nailed to the mustard-green shingles: "Pat King Real Estate: For Sale."

Thomas was in this house one spring day in 1976 when a message came from the Liberal MLA for Bridgewater, Dr. Maurice DeLory, who was by now the minister of tourism. Would Thomas come to his office? "I was a Liberal at the time," says Thomas, "so I went." DeLory asked him to go to Philadelphia and take over *Bluenose II*.

"I know nothing about sailing ships," Thomas protested. "I know they sail, that's all. I don't like to take command of the ship when I don't even know the terminology."

DeLory persisted. Without a certified skipper — whether knowledgeable in sail or not — the ship would not be allowed in New York's Operation Sail. Thomas conceded that Nova Scotia, and Canada, would miss a great opportunity if *Bluenose II* were forced out of the parade of tall ships, and he finally agreed — on the understanding that he would be along essentially to make things legal, that the other officers would do the sailing and that he would be relieved when the ship reached Halifax. But he was not relieved, and in the meantime he missed his other opportunities to go back to sea. He stayed on as skipper for another season, resigning largely because he felt the ship was being poorly run and he was powerless to do anything about it. His charges provoked a noisy public debate with Maurice DeLory.

"*Bluenose II* is no place for a man who's been skipper of a ship before," Thomas argues. "It's a government ship. Nobody gives a damn. When you work in a commercial ship, the ship has to make money for its owners. If it doesn't, you're gone. Your job's on the line every single day. I've worked all afternoon at my desk about the crew's overtime and the net result was to save D. K. Ludwig thirty-five cents."

D. K. Ludwig is the New York shipping magnate whose personal wealth — $3 billion, Thomas says — entitles him to be considered perhaps the richest man in the world. He didn't get there by overlooking thirty-five cents here and there. Shipping is not a game, or an art. It is one of the coldest businesses on earth. Shipowners — "international carnivores," as one lawyer calls them — traditionally cut corners everywhere, skimp on safety, transfer ships from one paper company to another, from one flag of convenience to another, all in search of maximum profit at minimum cost. Immense fortunes have been made in shipping — ask Jacqueline Onassis — but not by sailors.

Andrew Thomas worked all his life in conditions of tedium and isolation, skippering mammoth tankers from Curaçao to New York, from Peru to Japan to the Persian Gulf, from the Persian Gulf to Europe. Thomas produces some tattered photos of ships he commanded: bald, gigantic, functional containers of oil, with enough attributes of a ship to make them self-propelled. On the European run, the ship would take a month to reach the Persian Gulf. It would load at an offshore terminal, often out of sight of land. It would sail another month to get home and unload at another offshore terminal. After nine continuous months, the skipper would get a month of leave. At each end of the voyage, there would be a flurry of frantic activity — customs, crew changes, provisioning, and the like. Between ports, the mates stood the watches, while the engineers ran the engine rooms. The skipper had nothing to do.

"I used to answer my mail," Thomas says. "I would open one letter every day and answer it. Or I would do one piece of washing, by hand. That way, I could feel I had done *something* that day. Oh, you're lonely, you're lonely." His crews were mostly from the Cayman or Cape Verde islands. Occasionally a compatible American would turn up as chief engineer. Otherwise, tanker crews are picked up wherever labour is cheap. A Finnish captain might have an all-Greek crew or a Korean crew. You're lonely, you're lonely.

A decade ago a company doctor diagnosed high blood pressure and sent Thomas home. No more would he command these modern leviathans. He would take seven different pills a day, occasionally delivering a trawler from Europe to Nova Scotia or a survey vessel from Capetown to Galveston via the Falklands and Brazil. He would suffer a stroke, the after-effects of which still show slightly in his speech.

And he would be plunged into the work of a government P.R. ship, dealing with scores of tourists every day, making round-trip voyages to the harbour mouth and back. The traditions he was raised in — discipline, order, frugality, the isolation of command — would become largely irrelevant. The government would squander money on food and laundry, and the firing of a crewman would be a problem of politics or public relations. Plans would be changed on the whim of the premier. The "receptions" for distinguished guests often became, in Thomas's eyes, little more than hard-drinking parties for cabinet ministers.

"I took the ship into Lunenburg," Thomas says. "It's her home port, and she hadn't been there for a long time. I held a little reception for people that were associated with her, like Spike Walters. It wasn't a partisan affair. I was told the government didn't want any parties there because Lunenburg had a Tory member. And I shouldn't have had Spike Walters aboard either, because Spike is a prominent Tory."

Thomas was the third professional skipper to leave *Bluenose II* under government ownership, and he feels a deep sense of affront to his calling. All three masters, he says, left in a cloud of bitterness and recrimination, all three had their professional reputations somehow besmirched by their association with *Bluenose II*. And what for? Because they had tried to run the ship in the way they had learned a ship should be run.

His children are grown and gone. He and his wife have separated. He lives in this echoing house with a bull terrier named Whisky. The house costs $1,200 a year to heat, and with the proceeds from its sale he could live forever in an apartment in Chester. He would like to go back to sea again, as a mate or a relief skipper.

He stands in the doorway with Whisky as I walk away in the twilight — a solitary, awkward man on the threshold of old age.

You're lonely, you're lonely.

Friday — Noon Watch

Don Barr is edgy. The channel into Atlantic City is only eighteen feet deep at low water and *Bluenose II* draws nearly sixteen feet. She churns up mud even in Lunenburg Harbour, which is badly silted. If a swell is running when we go into Atlantic City, she could bounce her keel on the bottom.

"We may not be able to go in at all," Barr declares. "We might have to go straight on to Norfolk."

The watch begins, as Rick Moore says, "T'ick, t'ick, t'ick o' fog," but it burns off steadily as the northwesterly breeze fills in. Four-foot seas slap the black hull. Visibility rises to seven miles. The schooner wallows along doing three or four knots, sixty miles east-northeast of Atlantic City.

In 1978 the Liberals were defeated. Lunenburg's Tory MLA, Bruce Cochran, turned up in the new cabinet and he hired Peter Brown. Don Barr got his master's ticket, and took over command of *Bluenose II*. The Gilbert and Sullivan period came to an end.

Barr grew up all over Canada, but he is firmly settled in Nova Scotia. He has been with the ship for ten years. He must be almost unique in having almost all his sea-time in sail. He loves to sail. His idea of a vacation is to go sailing. Along with two friends, he is building a fleet of three identical daysailers in his barn. (He is also building a fiberglass replica of a 1929 Mercedes Benz there. He is impatient with cars that cost twelve thousand dollars and rust out in three years.) Above all, his personality is perfect for the job. He is tolerant, talkative, and gregarious. He runs the ship with easy-natured informality. At the same time, he is firmly in charge. I feel sure, too, that he has a temper, and on the rare occasions when he loses it, I think I would like to be in Alberta.

Barr has surrounded himself with a permanent crew who are friends as well as colleagues, who share his devotion to the ship, and who understand her work. All the deck officers have been aboard for at least four years. Between them and the government stands Peter Brown who shares their determination that the ship shall be a credit to Nova Scotia, answerable to the politicians but run in a crisply professional style. Politics have not become irrelevant, of course. Barr and Brown require four experienced deckhands each season and eight green ones. They conduct interviews and make up a short list. The minister makes the final selection. The minister's criteria are not known. This is Nova Scotia, however. It is unlikely that he takes the opportunity to encourage his opponents.

So the crew are presumably of sound Tory stock, or at least not opposed to the Tories. David Stevens, indeed, has been nicknamed "Tory" for his family's unshakable party loyalty. But at least the hands are competent, suitable Tories, and if they cannot do the work, they are fired.

Ron Ottens comes on deck. Both engines are idling over. The batteries are still very low and the electronic equipment is being used sparingly. But, says Ron, "if the old man wants power for going through that cut, he's got it."

The ship's mechanical systems, Ron says, are excellently planned but somewhat outdated. "Those fuel filters were the state of the art when the ship was built. Today, they came over with Noah. There's a few changes to make in the layout of the hydraulics, too. I'll fix some of those things up this fall. I can afford the time. I want to keep this job. With this job, I can keep on going to school, so it's worth making the effort. The engine layout is the same as the original *Bluenose*, did you know that?

"It's funny, they've spent very little money in the engine room. But after twenty years, it needs a little attention. The engine room is the heart of the ship. The brain may run things, but only as long as the heart is pumping blood. Without that generator you can't eat, you can't have lights, you can't shit, you can't raise the sails, and you can't drop the anchor.

"Something I really appreciate — the crew on this ship will pitch right in to help the engineer. I've been on lots of ships where people would laugh — there's the engineer working his butt off, haha — but on this ship there's none of that. The night before we left, when we had trouble with the bilge pumps, Billy and Delbé and Ricky and me all worked together, and we proved the whole system right up to the ejectors, and the next day we could just say to the shipyard boys, there's the problem, take it off. And we were right. We knew. That whole night, I never laid a wrench on it myself. They wanted me around to help figure it out, but they did it. There aren't too many crews like that. Pure gold, twenty-four carat."

Don Barr is still considering the swell, which hasn't gone down much. In fact, as we close the coast and the water gradually shoals, the swells pile up more steeply, come closer together. Barr is faintly nervous. He was aboard *Bluenose II* during the comic-opera period, and he knows the snares and traps that await even the most prudent mariner. This new port is a new set of circumstances, and he is in charge of Nova Scotia's reputation as well as his own.

Meanwhile, all through the ship, men are taking cold showers — Ron hasn't yet got enough power to turn on the water heaters — and shaving and breaking out clean shirts. How many eligible women are there in Atlantic City?

"Channel fever," smiles Wayne Walters. "All hands preparing to pillage and plunder."

Close to the major U.S. ports, the traffic is becoming heavy. A tug and its tow appear off the bow, plodding out to sea. After supper, the horizon is crowded with tugs and tows — long oil barges, many of them, used in shallow creeks and rivers. Barr remarks that these barges are frequent all down the U.S. coast, though for some reason they are not often seen in the Maritimes. Around us now, five or six tugs are plugging along on a confusing welter of courses, some with two tows, apparently immobile and yet changing their bearings constantly. Far off to starboard is the hulking shape of a container vessel, steering to cross ahead of us. To port on the horizon, a husky orange ship is growing larger, preparing to cross astern. The orange ship comes closer until with binoculars one can make out the words painted in immense white letters on her top-sides: *Barber Blue Line.*

"One of the biggest shipping companies in the States," says Barr. "Funny that they call it 'Blue Line' and paint their ships orange."

As the Barber ship steams past our stern, Wayne Walters claps the binoculars to his eyes, training them on the distant ship to starboard.

"I've never seen one loaded like that," he comments. "Containers right to the bridge."

As the ship comes on we can all see what he means. The ship is big, grey, utilitarian, with containers looking like a child's blocks piled up right beneath the windows of the pilothouse. She looks like a housewife's iron upside down, with a pronounced slope up from bow to stern. She passes close ahead, forging steadily down the coast.

Barr suddenly invites Delbé and me below to his snug cabin next to the engine room. By some democratic subsection of Murphy's Law, the noise of the engines is strong in here and strongest of all precisely in Barr's own berth. He returns a book to me: *Two Sailors*, a children's book by Warwick Tompkins about his family's 1936 passage from Gloucester to San Francisco via Cape Horn aboard *Wanderbird*, the family's converted North Sea pilot schooner. Barr, Brown, and I share an enthusiasm for Tompkins, and now Barr says again how pleased he is to hear that *Wanderbird*, after years as a mastless houseboat in Sausalito, is being rebuilt and prepared again for sea.

Barr wishes *Bluenose II* would make more trips, and longer ones. When he first joined her, she worked eight months a year. Now it's down to about five months, and the ports visited are too often the same ones. Atlantic City, in fact, is the only new port on this cruise. There is a tension here between the ship and the government. Peter Brown has told me about an offer by an English foundation to charter the ship and her crew, take her to England, give her a complete refit, send her on a cruise around the world in the wake of Sir Francis Drake, put her through another refit on her return, send her home to Nova Scotia — and pay a

$2 million charter fee, which would be enough to build another schooner from scratch, if need be. The government refused, preferring to keep her in Halifax for harbour cruises. Brown would have taken the offer in a flash, using the trip to promote Nova Scotia all around the world.

Her annual routine now begins with a tour to the U.S. east coast in April and May, followed by two months of Halifax harbour tours. In 1981 she varied this routine by revisiting the Great Lakes much more successfully than in 1975. In September she visits Lunenburg for the Fisheries Exhibition, and often during the fall she travels to other Nova Scotian ports — Pictou, Sydney, Port Hawkesbury, Sheet Harbour, Shelburne, Yarmouth — for local festivals and fairs. By late October she is laid up in Lunenburg, generally at the museum wharf, and the crew disperses for the winter.

This routine makes sense, and much business is done on these tours. In Toronto, for instance, in 1981, the ship took a party of travel agents for a sail. In the salon, tourism officials had literature and videotapes of Nova Scotia, details of hotels and tourist attractions. On that one brief excursion they sold $3.5 million worth of 1982 rooms to tourbus operators and other agents. Similarly, in Boston a sail aboard *Bluenose II* allowed M.L.W. Worthington, a Montreal firm owned by Bombardier, to close a $50 million deal to provide rolling stock for Amtrak. These charters themselves are often paid for by the Canadian consuls in the various cities, and between charters and tours the ship actually covers her own costs on these voyages. The income from the Halifax tours alone almost always covers her operating expenses and routine maintenance, though it does not cover such major outlays as the cost of last winter's refit.

The ship's reputation prompted Walt Disney Productions to make a twenty-minute Circlevision film in Lunenburg in 1981, showing *Bluenose II* leaving the Fisheries Museum under full sail. The film will be shown thirty-five times a day for ten years at Disney World in Orlando,

Florida — an enviable promotion for the town and the province.

So the ship is being intelligently and productively used. Barr and Brown simply suspect that bolder strokes might bring bigger gains. There is a whole world out there for the taking.

Barr produces an Aero mint bar and breaks it in pieces.

"I wish I could offer you something stronger," he grins. On this voyage, at least, *Bluenose II* has been an utterly dry ship. Not so much as a beer has been served. Barr and Brown are both sensitive about alcohol since heavy drinking and empty beer bottles caused so much trouble earlier in the ship's life. The recommissioning party just before we left Lunenburg was a rare exception to the ship's abstemious habits. In Halifax, *Bluenose II* is berthed at Privateer's Wharf on which there is both a tavern and a lounge. Drunken boarding parties often issue forth at closing time with the notion of climbing the rigging, diving off the bowsprit, or taking the ship for a sail. One determined woman brought Norman Whynot to the deck with a flying tackle while the rest of her party poured over the gangplank. Wayne Walters has occasionally used the fire hose to repel winous boarders. The current solution is a special gangplank built by Bill Lutwick, which is raised by a halyard at nine p.m. like a drawbridge. It leaves a ten-foot space of open water between the ship and the pier.

It has been a long battle to restore the ship's reputation, to instill pride in her crew and make her a fitting representative of a proud old province. Liquor, particularly, can only hurt her. The battle suffered a setback in 1982 when a friend of a deckhand staggered aboard in the final stages of drunkenness looking for his friend's company in a pubcrawl. His friend refused and asked for permission to put the man to bed in the ship, out of harm's way. This is against the ship's policy, but it seemed brutal to turn the man out on the street in that condition. During the night, however, he vomited and failed to turn his face. They found him suffocated in the morning, and the story was around Halifax like a prairie fire, producing another round of stories about drunken parties in the fo'c'sle.

By contrast, the *National Enquirer* that same year called the crew of *Bluenose II* "snobs" because they had laughed at the U.S. Coast Guard training ship *Eagle*. *Bluenose II* was sailing up the Delaware River under full canvas while *Eagle* was motoring like the other Tall Ships bound for Philadelphia's Parade of Sail. "Sure, we were laughing," smiles David Stevens. "Wouldn't you? Call themselves sailors — !"

And now, while we are discussing these things comfortably in Don Barr's cabin, a voice on deck calls, "We have a landfall!" We hear rushing feet, people running on deck. Don Barr grins. "Their first foreign landfall. Pretty exciting for them."

"Mine, too," I observe.

"Is it? Oh, well, let's go on deck."

Wayne Walters is smiling as we reach the companionway.

"It's actually more of a building-fall," he explains. "What you can see is the high-rises. You can't actually see the shore yet."

Sure enough, there they are, the rectangles of downtown Atlantic City faint in the golden evening haze ahead.

A cluster of young men gathers on the foredeck, chatting excitedly, passing binoculars around. *Bluenose II* putters along over an almost calm sea, swinging behind a tug towing two barges, as the coast slowly shows its features. There's a water tower. Two water towers. Houses, low along the beach. A big sailboat drives to windward, her taut sails cutting across the building faces like the curving edge of a knife. As we draw slowly nearer, we can see that she is a big varnished sloop with a three-quarter rig and a spoon bow — an outdated racer, by the looks of her.

"She looks like an old twelve-meter," Barr suggests.

Other tall ships arriving early would go in and tie up, and then sail out again in the morning for the parade. *Bluenose II* prefers to make a grand entrance precisely when the parade lines up, so we have sixteen hours to kill. Barr keeps on coming in, picking up one navigational buoy after another, calling on the radio to *Young America*, the hundred-foot ferrocement brigantine-rigged training ship which makes her home in Atlantic City and which will be the host ship for tomorrow's parade. Barr wants to get in touch with Peter Brown, Norman Whynot, and Peter's associate Pat Martin, nicknamed "Keychains" because he's in charge of souvenir sales. Barr also wants to confirm the depths in the channel.

Young America reassures him about the channel but has heard nothing from Brown. By now the sun has fallen behind the high-rises and the ship has reached the last buoy before the harbour. Lights and neon signs glow along the boardwalk, near enough to read with the naked eye. Golden Nugget. Resorts. And yes, that is the Playboy Bunny, outlined in white neon on the corner of a blocky hotel.

Bluenose II does a tight circle around the inner buoy and heads out to sea again.

"I hate it when he does this," grins Rick Moore. "Comes in so close you can taste it, and then heads out to sea again."

As we turn towards the seaward blackness, the top corner blows off the Playboy Hotel, a brilliant orange explosion with rolling clouds of smoke. Then wheels of fire erupt in the sky, rockets scream upwards and burst, silver fountains cascade off the rooftops. This is the Memorial Day weekend in Atlantic City, and the fireworks will go on for the best part of an hour.

Wayne Walters glances seaward and cries, "Look!"

A single scarlet spot, brilliant against the black sky, falls slowly towards the open ocean. A red flare. A distress signal.

"Parachute flare," says Don Barr. "Get a bearing on it. Look, there goes another one. Bring her around till she's heading for that flare. Get a couple of men in the bow for lookouts. Gordie. Ian. Wayne, call the Coast Guard. Tell 'em what we saw and let 'em know we're heading out there. See if you can find anything on the radar."

The radio squawks. The sailing vessel *American Eagle*, off Atlantic City, reports red flares to the Coast Guard. "There you are," says Barr. "She was an old twelve-meter. She used to be owned by Ted Turner, I think."

Engines drumming, *Bluenose II* heads seaward. The ride in the bow is spectacular, as a big copper moon rises and the schooner, moving at eight knots, rises over the swells and tramples down in a smother of foam, sheets of spray flashing out from her cheeks. The sea is dark, with cubist planes of moonlit water appearing and dissolving, black hollows promising everything and yielding nothing. The men's eyes sweep the dark and ambiguous surface. The intercom under the breasthook crackles.

"See anything up there?"

"Nothing yet."

"No target on the radar, either."

The bow rises and falls like an enormous romping horse. No one speaks. A rescue at sea would provide a spectacular conclusion to the voyage and a dramatic introduction to Atlantic City. By now, though, we should surely have sighted whatever there might be to see.

It would not be *Bluenose II*'s first rescue. Several times she has sighted small vessels in distress, standing by until the Coast Guard arrived. Once the vessel was a Halifax yacht that had been stolen by a group of very young boys who found themselves unable to handle her and were drifting onto McNabs Island, in the mouth of Halifax Harbour, when *Bluenose II* came by on the way in from a harbour cruise.

On September 9, 1978, Don Barr was coming back on deck facing astern when he thought he saw a red flare. Nobody else was looking that way but Barr put the ship about anyway. A few moments later another flare went up, and this time everyone saw it. It was a dirty night with a thirty-five-knot southeasterly blowing the sea into serrate ridges. Barr called Halifax Traffic, twenty miles away, and asked that the Coast Guard be notified. Halifax called Sambro twenty miles down the coast, and the forty-four-foot rescue boat *Coast Guard 117* was at sea five minutes later.

Bluenose II swept down on the scene and found the distressed vessel — a forty-two-foot orange-hulled fishing boat out of Blandford by the name of *Julie and Brothers*. Her engine was dead, she was taking on water, and her crew had been preparing to abandon her. The big schooner stood by, ready to take them off if necessary.

Coast Guard 117 arrived, after a fast and wet run from Sambro, pitching fiercely and rolling her cabin sides into the water. She floated a pump and a towline down to *Julie and Brothers*. The pump started to empty the fishing boat, and *Coast Guard 117* took up the strain on the towline. *Bluenose II* motored to windward of the two small vessels shielding them from the worst of the wind and sea until they found smoother water near the land. Then the schooner bore away for Sydney, and more harbour tours.

Gordie, Ian, and I stand silent in the bow, imagining heroic rescues. The fireworks of Atlantic City recede in the distance. And then the intercom crackles again:

"Come on back here."

A U.S. Navy ship, far over the horizon, fired the flares in a spasm of patriotic fervour, in honour of Memorial Day. Disdainful of civilians, she neglected to notify the Coast Guard or other ships.

No matter. We had nothing better to do. *Bluenose II* settles down into a fast idle, preparing to while away the night. Down in the fo'c'sle, the hands are playing cribbage and going through a girlie magazine like farm women with a mail-order catalogue.

"Now there's a nice one."

"Too big, too big."

"We're all suffering from DSB."

"DSB?"

"Deadly Sperm Buildup."

It's a raunchy evening. Just over there on the horizon is one of America's play capitals, a mass of sand beaches, summer hotels, casinos, nightclubs. Just imagine the thousands of nubile American girls, humid at the prospect of a salty Bluenose seaman.

"My deah," says Rick Moore, mimicking an American woman, "he was from Nova Scotia, that's — I don't know, in Canada, I think — and he was so *very* eager...."

Behind all the bravado and locker-room humour lies an archetypal reality. These young men, almost alone in their generation of Nova Scotians, have made an ocean passage under sail. They are bigger, more capable, than they were in Lunenburg. Who knows what inner seas of apprehension, fear, and self-doubt they may have crossed? They have become part of a fraternity that includes the most revered touchstones of their culture. They feel their manhood enhanced, and the confirmation of manhood is given by women. There is always something moving about the transformation of boys into men, and it has advanced perceptibly in the last five days.

A voyage takes place inside us, too.

Saturday — Graveyard Watch

Fifteen miles off the distant glitter of Atlantic City, *Bluenose II* jogs around a great triangle. This is a busy stretch of ocean crisscrossed by myriad ships and boats. The night is clear and the lights come and go across the face of the sea. With binoculars, one can just make out the hulking mass of a container ship, the low black smudge of a barge.

"Tug," says Delbé, putting down the glasses. "Tow over six hundred feet long."

"How can you tell?" asks Brian.

"Three white lights in line on the mast," says Delbé. "Two, if the tow is under six hundred feet. Take her twenty-five degrees to starboard."

"Twenty-five degrees to starboard," Brian repeats, swinging the wheel and squinting at the compass. The International Regulations for the Prevention of Collision at Sea, or COLREGS as they are known, require "positive early action" where a risk of collision exists. If you alter course, you make a big alteration, so that no doubt can remain about what you are doing. This is a good night for brushing up on COLREGS, or learning them — lots of shipping, and a night so calm and clear that one can see for miles.

"For some of these big ships, six miles is considered 'close quarters'," Delbé comments. "They take several miles to stop. When I altered course, we were about three miles from that container ship over there, and I imagine the third officer was beginning to think about altering course himself or calling the old man."

Third officer?

"This is the third officer's shift," Delbé explains. It is therefore the most dangerous shift. A startling 45 percent of ship accidents occur when the youngest least-experienced and least-qualified ship's deck officer is on watch. Delbé had this watch before Rick Moore became third mate. In those days, the captain himself stood a watch and Delbé was the most junior officer. Now Barr stands no regular watch and Delbé could hand this watch to Rick, but he likes it.

"It fouls up my sleeping habits all winter, though," he smiles. "It's the one big problem between me and Mary. When I wake up, I can't just lie there. I have to read, or watch TV or something. If she's really tired she'll go back to sleep, but otherwise I have to go out to the living room till I get tired again.

"You know, when I was a deckhand, I would just about go to sleep on the wheel on this watch. When I went below I'd go right to sleep. Now I can't. The officer has to be alert all the time, watching the situation and checking courses. Look in towards Atlantic City. There's a ship in there, see it? I only saw it now. It was hidden among the lights ashore, and I didn't notice it until I happened to see its lights moving. That's the kind of thing that's an officer's responsibility. "

My trick at the wheel. I look affectionately at the ship I am guiding, recalling David Stevens's grandfather's remark that a ship is more like a living thing than anything else a man can make with his hands and that it is therefore a joy and a privilege to be a shipbuilder, a creator of such lovely vital beings. Tomorrow I will leave her, and I will find it hard to do.

I will find it hard to give up these dark watches, too, which draw the five men so strongly together, bring them to talk so openly and powerfully about their feelings, their sense of their own lives. Delbé, for example, has hold me he was almost in despair when he joined the ship, having been driven to the conclusion that he would never find an occupation that would satisfy him and that he could work at with devotion for the rest of his life. The three younger men are softer and more malleable in their characters, responsible and serious almost to a fault, an easy prey for guilt and uncertainty. Their identities are still slightly fuzzy, which is part of the charm of youth, part of what keeps teachers content with their profession. In spirit, though, these crewmen all seem much older than the captain.

I am steering for Atlantic City now, on a landward leg of our aimless course. Our port of destination could hardly be more different from our port of departure. Atlantic City is John Kenneth Galbraith's "private splendour and public squalour" made manifest. Along the shoreline runs the boardwalk, a forty-foot width of yellow pine planks soaked in pentachlorophenol, nearly six miles long, with expanses of sand on one side and extravagant hotels on the other. There are nine glittering casinos — vast caverns of slot machines, baccarat, blackjack, roulette. The mood is grim and serious in the casinos. Middle-aged women in flowered dresses, cigarettes dangling from the corners of their mouths, hold plastic cups filled with half-dollars, pumping one coin after another into the slot machines. Now and then the machine disgorges a shower of coins into the cast-aluminum trays at their waists. The women do not even look down. They have already inserted another coin, they have already pulled the handle again. Silver domes inverted on the ceiling conceal TV surveillance. A rock band plays furiously on a stage at one end of the casino. Nobody is listening. In a central atrium, leafy and rough cast, fat men and plastic women get together over drinks. A jazz trio plays elegant and easy. Nobody listens to them, either.

Atlantic City's casinos are chiefly along the boardwalk. A block away, on Pacific Avenue, pawnshops jostle with cigar stores. Six blocks inland, ten blocks inland, following North Carolina Avenue, States Avenue, Virginia, Kentucky, is terminal urban rot. Apartment buildings, charming old brick homes, squat bungalows, shops, offices — abandoned, deserted, boarded up. Packs of dogs move hungrily through broken glass and grassy patches where buildings once stood. Black children play baseball in the ruined streets. Beyond Pacific Avenue, Atlantic City is chiefly ghetto. The contrasts are shocking. One block is inhabited, with mown lawns and fresh paint and flowering trees. The next block is a war zone of blank-eyed buildings and twisted fencing. Canada has its streets of despair, but we have nothing, anywhere, to compare with this bombed-out horror of a community.

If the street names sound familiar, it is because you once played Monopoly, a game created by one Charles B. Darrow (1889-1967) and based on Atlantic City. There is a plaque in his memory at the corner of — where else? — Boardwalk and Park Place. There is, indeed, a hotel at that corner. It is called Bally's, it includes a casino, and it is quite possible to lose your entire stake by landing on Boardwalk and Park Place. Monopoly is not merely a game. It is an accurate reflection of the America that created Atlantic City. The original Atlantic City, before the ghetto, was a highly exclusive resort, with leafy avenues and plane-trees, where tycoons arrived in private railway cars — Atlantic City exists because a railway terminated here and brought their horses in their private railway cars. Jack Dempsey trained here for his fight with Gene Tunney. John Philip Sousa marched his band down the boardwalk. Al Capone favoured the city as a site for his business meetings. Monopoly, all right. You do not want to own Mediterranean and Baltic. They are the main streets of the ghetto.

Delbé Comeau has a book in his cabin by Alain Colas. The book is in French. Colas was a famous ocean-racing singlehander who disappeared at sea during the 1978 singlehanded transatlantic race — an expansive, lighthearted, laughing man, by all accounts, greatly mourned in yachting circles.

"I met him," Delbé says when I mention the book. "He was aboard the ship in 1976, in New York. His boat, Club Med, was berthed just ahead of us after Operation Sail. I was amazed — he knew all about this ship, all about the original *Bluenose*, her racing record and everything. We had a long talk. He was pleased to find a crew member who could speak French with him. He laughed a lot because I don't know the French words for nautical things. I've only served on English-speaking ships.

"He said he'd heard about the *Bluenose* all his life and he was thrilled to be aboard her. It was one of his life's dreams to see her and go aboard, and he had realized it. I was surprised. I didn't know she was that famous, not outside North America."

Delbé got Colas's book from a young French couple in a twenty-five-foot aluminum sloop who passed through Halifax on their way home after a classical circular tour of the North Atlantic — south to the trade winds, west to the Caribbean, north to New England and Nova Scotia, home in the westerlies above the 40th parallel. They, too, were pleased to find an Acadian mate on the schooner, and they, too, had made Halifax a port of call in part because of *Bluenose II*. Later, they sent Delbé some scrimshaw from the Azores and after they reached France they sent him the Colas book.

"They also sent me this," grins Delbé, handing over another book.

It's a nautical dictionary. In six languages.

Saturday — Arrival

The Parade of Sail begins off Million Dollar Pier at twelve o'clock Atlantic City time, which is one o'clock Lunenburg time. We have not changed the ship's clocks. The parade will fall plumb in the middle of our watch.

We are still well offshore this sunny morning. When I come on deck at eleven o'clock, the four lowers are set and drawing to a light southeasterly, and men are at the mastheads, loosening the brailing lines on the gaff topsails. With a thundering sound of running feet, half a dozen men charge aft with the tail of the balloon jib halyard, sending the sail flying to the peak of the foremast. From the depths of the hull, the fisherman staysail is being fed to the deck crew. This is the first time we have seen it. At 1,900 square feet, it is the ship's second largest sail.

On the roof of the deckhouse stands a husky little bronze cannon in a meticulous carriage, a three-pounder cast in the Lunenburg Foundry for Wayne Walters. It fires tea bags filled with black powder lit by a proper fuse through a little touchhole. Wayne catches me examining it and grins.

"Cap'n Sinbad's going to be in the parade," he says. "We'll have to be ready for him."

Cap'n Horatio Sinbad is a legendary character in these events. With his wife and two children, he sails a minuscule brigantine. *Meka II* is just thirty-six feet on deck, despite her painted gunports and profusion of gear. His family wears wide canvas pants, striped shirts, and bandannas. They support themselves by offering educational cruises for young people, concentrating on piracy, privateering, and sixteenth and seventeenth-century British naval practices. The little ship boasts square sails on the foremast, including a triangular raffee at the masthead. The binnacle is brass. The rigging is adjusted with deadeyes and lanyards, not with turnbuckles. The wheel is a proper wooden ship's wheel, spokes and all.

"Oh, he's really into it," chuckles Don Barr. "As far as he's concerned, it's 1750 at the latest."

The fisherman staysail goes fluttering aloft and is sheeted home. With every stitch of canvas set, *Bluenose II* strides easily along. She ignores the virtual absence of wind. Fat little sports fishermen, racy runabouts, and cabin cruisers come out to meet us, their owners snapping photographs.

She must look wonderful in their viewfinders, glistening with fresh paint and polished brass, clouds of sail aloft, her crew in matched slacks and T-shirts. My trick at the wheel, and I contemplate that white expanse of canvas above me and the little ships now beginning to gather around us. Crabbers and clammers, tiny cruisers, big ketches, a steel schooner. A couple of daring Hobie cats, a squat tugboat, a dragger or two. A huge, old open sloop, badly hogged, named *Helena G. Starn*, which sports a jazzy rainbow mainsail emblazoned with the word *Harrah's* — one of the main casinos.

Remember it. Savour it. You have taken the helm of this mythic schooner on a proud, showy day, when she is creaming along with all sail set. Remember what it feels like, the grainy oaken spokes of the wheel in your hand, the slight cant to the deck, the sense of pride and power. There is nothing here to touch her. She is the queen of this parade. We are a privileged few, those of us alive today who have handled the wheel of a Banks schooner under a full press of sail, those who have come so near the heart of a great legend of our country.

David Stevens relieves me and we fall in behind *Young America*. The ships cluster beside us and behind us: *Meka II, Yankee, Ada Adelia, M.L. Wescoat,* a J30, a Riva 60, a Stiletto catamaran, a plug-ugly U.S. Navy ROTC centre-cockpit ketch called *Rainbeau,* a lean and missile-like Cigarette.

"Down south, they call that a smuggler's boat," confides Don Barr. "You can get them as long as seventy feet, with four V-8's in them."

Overhead, a light plane trails a message behind it: PHIL'S ROCK ROOM. Another plane crosses our bow: ADULT ENTERTAINMENT GIRLS 345-5400. Power cruisers with cutesy names wallow beside us: *Fracture II, Knot Deductible*. In a low blue runabout, a rival of Dolly Parton stands and shakes her ample bosom at our crew, who whistle and cheer.

"Take it off!"

"Give us a look!"

To our surprise, she does, revealing five-gallon storage tanks to port and starboard. A tawny, hairy-chested man in a nearby boat laughs, waving at this awesome spectacle.

"Welcome to Atlantic City!"

Meka II pulls up beside us, the Jolly Roger streaming out behind her. CRACK! and a puff of smoke. Cap'n Sinbad has fired a three-pound bow chaser mounted on a circular carriage. Wayne Walters steps up to his bronze cannon and touches a match to the fuse. With a deafening BANG! the cannon belches smoke. A tea bag hits the water fifty feet away. Another report and a puff of smoke from *Young America*. Cap'n Sinbad trumps us all: he has two one-pound stern swivels as well as his bow chaser and he now fires all three. Bang-bang-BANG! Wayne fires our cannon again and again. The sound richochets and echoes among the tall buildings, swirls around the sands. Ashore, on the boardwalk Peter Brown laughs to see the people come running, attracted by the cannonade.

Wayne Walters ducks below and speaks into the VHF radio. *Young America* is motoring, wearing perhaps half her sail — a jib, her forecourse, a staysail, her spanker. Now she belches exhaust from her topsides and suddenly speeds up. Wayne smiles at Ron and Rick. Ron winks at Delbé. Delbé smiles at Don.

The sun pours down on Don Barr, his feet spread wide on his quarterdeck, his gold stripes bright on his epaulets, a broad and mischievous smile splitting his open, happy face. He knows what Wayne said to the American brigantine.

Like *Young America, Bluenose II* is using her engines to keep station in the parade. She is using quite a lot of power. Her engines are at half-throttle.

In *reverse.*

Epilogue: Cycles of Schooners

Nine years pass like a wink. On another May morning on the Lunenburg waterfront, the schooner readies herself for another departure. This time she is bound for Halifax en route to Quebec, Montreal, Toronto and way points, celebrating Canada's 125th birthday — an ambiguous anniversary, if ever there was one. As she sails, another deadline approaches in the constitutional debate, and an inconclusive conference of first ministers convenes every week in a different corner of the country to consider whether Canada's provinces will continue to function as one nation.

Bluenose II lies at the Scotia Trawler wharf in the warm sunshine, her stern beyond the end of the wharf, her bowsprit reaching for the beach. A dozen young people in blue shorts and white shirts are snapping on the dory covers, coiling down lines, carrying boxes of stores down the varnished gangplank, standing by the docklines. Lulu and I are joining her just for the day, sailing to Halifax on the first leg of her voyage.

A sandy-haired man in sunglasses stands on the wharf, gazing down at the ship, scanning her from end to end. Peter Brown. He looks up, sees his visitors, grins, and enfolds them in a hug as large and warm as a wool blanket. A car pulls up, and Don Barr ambles down the wharf, a big smiling man in a short-sleeved white shirt, enjoying the scene, the sunlight, the resumption of the ship's travels.

We follow Barr down the gangplank. A bulky figure waves from the engine control box. Ron Ottens. A slight, bearded man is supervising the work of a gang of young people. Delbé Comeau. A quick grin, a fast firm handshake. Peter, Don, Ron, Delbé: it's like coming home.

The ship glistens with fresh paint and varnish. Brilliant black, stinging white, deep rusty-red mahogany, yellow Douglas fir. This spring was snowy and bitterly cold, with ice in Lunenburg Harbour a month later than usual, so the shipyard workers and the crew have been working furiously to get the work done during brief interludes of warmth. The varnish, they say, wasn't spread on the wood; it froze to the wood.

"You've heard about chilled varnish?" grins Delbé.

"Yeah —?"

"Well, this is a new technology," says Delbé. "Now we chill the ship, not the varnish."

Delbé is first mate now; Wayne Walters is skippering gypsum vessels from Nova Scotia to the eastern U.S. Rick Moore has swallowed the anchor and taken a job with the housing authority. The new second mate is Marty Murrin, a dark-haired, serious young man from Antigonish; the third mate is Phil Watson, from nearby Mahone Bay.

We go below through the saloon to the galley, which is generating a lusty aroma of beef stew. A short grey-haired man, dressed in white, is chopping and boiling and mixing. Noble Gignac: good old Gigs. A personable young woman with curly brown hair offers coffee and introduces herself: Jean Farrell is Gigs' steward, one of several young women in the crew. In recent years, *Bluenose II* has abandoned one of the most hoary and nasty of nautical traditions, the one which holds that women are bad luck aboard a ship.

Coffee in hand, I peruse the bulkheads in the saloon: plaques from San Francisco, Tampa, Vancouver, Miami, Savannah, Puget Sound. Since I sailed with her in 1983, *Bluenose II* has made regular calls to New England and the mid-Atlantic states, visiting six times in the past nine years — in 1984 and 1985, and again each year from 1987 to 1990. In 1985, Prince Andrew sailed aboard her in Halifax, and she was in Saint John, New Brunswick, for the Canada Games. In 1984, however, she also sailed to Bermuda to greet the Tall Ships as they assembled prior to eastern Canada's first-ever gathering of international sail-training ships. *Bluenose II* acted as Canada's host ship while the fleet visited Halifax, Quebec, and Sydney.

That summer was party time in the ports of Nova Scotia, the narrow streets and waterfront promenades of Halifax clogged with laughing young sailors from Poland, Spain, the Soviet Union, Colombia, the United States, Scandinavia, Argentina. One cloudless afternoon in July, I was on the end of a Halifax wharf serving as a TV commentator while the ships paraded up the Dartmouth side of Halifax Harbour, turned at the Macdonald Bridge and slowly cruised past downtown Halifax. At the head of the line was our own black schooner, leading them seaward and fading into the offshore haze. She looked dainty and almost ethereal in the company of the massive square-riggers.

In the saloon, Don Barr grins as he recalls that trip. In Bermuda, representatives from the Manoir Richelieu made the rounds of the tall ships, trying to persuade at least a few of them to stop at their grand hotel on the north shore of the St. Lawrence east of Quebec City. All but one declined. The exception was *Bluenose II*.

"The others didn't know how long it was going to take to get from Halifax to Quebec," Barr chuckles. "I knew. We had plenty of time. So I played a little bit hard-to-get, but at the last of it I said sure, we'd come. They gave us about the best dinner we ever got, didn't they?"

"It was fantastic," says Delbé Comeau, shaking his head.

"I think it was thirteen courses," Barr says. "Thirteen courses! The main course was duck, but they kept bringing soup and fish and all kinds of things. Really good, too. Then they finally brought the duck, and you know what it was? It was like a whole duck, baked inside something like a loaf of bread. One for each of us."

"The courses weren't that big, so you didn't get full," says Delbé. "But we weren't expecting a whole duck for each of us."

"It's a massive hotel," says Barr. "And the dining room where we ate is a glass room cantilevered out from the front of it, away up over the water. The rest of the ships went on by — it was raining, foggy. We sat there eating and most of them spent the night at anchor somewhere up the river. That was the best dinner anyone ever gave us."

Lulu and I were at the Coast Guard College in Sydney a month later when the fleet came back down the St. Lawrence — and that too was an amazing party, the walkways of the college lined with hot-pots and barbecues, Cape Breton girls laughing with South American cadets, music and dancing everywhere. Rock, swing, disco: just take your pick. And the next day the ships sailed slowly away, in a barely perceptible breeze. The sail training fleet was holding a race, with the finish line in Liverpool, England. *Bluenose II*, however, shaped her course southwest for Halifax.

In 1986, she made her most ambitious voyage: from Lunenburg to Vancouver for Expo 86 — the sort of voyage her managers always thought she should be taking. She left Nova Scotia in early December for Bermuda, where she spent the winter. In mid-February she sailed direct to Jamaica and the Panama Canal. She stopped briefly in Punta Arenas, Costa Rica; Acapulco, Mazatlan and San Carlos, Mexico; and San Diego, California, arriving in Los Angeles on April 1, in San Francisco on April 6, and in Victoria on April 17. She sailed on to Ladysmith and Nanaimo where "pirates" from the theatre department of Malaspina College captured and "tried" Don Barr for desertion: he had once lived in Nanaimo, but moved away around the age of eleven. She was in Vancouver at the end of April, ready for the opening of Expo 86 on May 2.

She did four main jobs in every port. As always, she spent many hours tied to the wharf while visitors trooped aboard. She took short cruises for local tourist wholesalers and travel "influencers," drumming up tourist business for Nova Scotia, and did similar sailings for guests with current or potential business interests in Nova Scotia. Smaller Nova Scotian companies invited West Coast dealers and distributors; federal and provincial trade officials courted investors, trading partners and possible new clients for the Port of Halifax.

By making a $1500 contribution to the Schooner Bluenose Foundation, larger corporations with a substantial presence in Nova Scotia could simply hire the vessel for a private sailing. Many did, including Moosehead, Maritime Life, Crossley-Karastan, National Sea Products, Stanfield's, Central Trust, Pratt and Whitney, Labatt's and the Bank of Nova Scotia.

After nearly two weeks in Vancouver, *Bluenose II* sailed on to Seattle before turning home. She called again at San

Francisco and Los Angeles, reached the Panama Canal on June 9, and made stops in Key West and Norfolk en route to New York. There she stayed a week, sailing in the Parade of Sail celebrating the centennial of the Statue of Liberty. After a stop in Boston, she sailed into Halifax on July 14.

In all the west coast ports, the big black schooner from the mysterious east had generated hordes of visitors and much admiring comment. Those who had visited her would remember their one concrete encounter with Nova Scotia, and if they remembered her as one San Francisco writer described her — "as trim as an aerobics teacher and smarter than a valedictorian" — then the trip had been a huge success.

Back in the ship's saloon, Don Barr shakes his head as he recalls the worst meal ever given by a host organization. The event occurred at an eastern U.S. port during one of the various gatherings of tall ships. The local committee had organized a "Captain's Breakfast" for all the skippers. The South Americans sported their most imposing finery: swords, whites, gold braid dripping from their hats and shoulders. Even Barr wore his dress uniform, with its stripes and scrambled eggs.

Limousines picked up the captains at the wharf, and drove them to an enormous nineteenth-century mansion on the waterfront — a robber baron's fantasy, now converted to public uses. The captains stood about and chatted with their hosts. In due course, uniformed maids bearing lidded silver dishes began circulating through the crowd asking whether the captains were ready to eat. They were. The maids lifted the lids of the silver dishes.

Each one held a cold Egg McMuffin in a styrofoam container.

Back on deck, Ron Ottens has the engines ticking over. The smell of diesel exhaust hangs in the warm, still air. Nine years later, Ron has the ship's mechanical systems ticking over smoothly. The engine room has been entirely re-done, engines overhauled, plumbing and wiring renewed, waste systems upgraded, new fuel tanks installed.

Ron stands at his control panel — an unobtrusive mahogany box with a Lexan lid, at the forward end of the deckhouse. Peter Brown goes ashore; he will meet the ship, as always, at her destination. Don Barr stands on the quarterdeck, issuing his commands with nods, hand signals and softly-spoken orders to the helmsman. He nods, and the stern line comes aboard. Another nod, and the bow line is cast off. A gesture to Ron, and the diesels rev up. *Bluenose II* slowly backs out into Lunenburg Harbour.

A long blast of a ship's horn echoes down the water. It comes from a big white brigantine moored at the Fisheries Museum wharf: the *Corwyn Cramer*, an oceanographic school ship from Wood's Hole, Massachusetts.

"Better give him a blast," mutters Barr, reaching into the companionway for the lanyard which releases a hoarse answering honk from the schooner's horn.

Bluenose II heads out of the harbour, past the National Sea plant and the long rocky spit with the lighthouse. She begins to feel the long rise and fall of the Atlantic swell. Marty Murrin and Phil Watson direct the crew as they haul on the web of blocks and lines. The sails rise, one after another: mainsail, foresail, jumbo, jib. It takes a while, and it is not done without some confusion: this is only the second time these young people have made sail aboard the schooner. Meanwhile the ship is motoring fast, knifing past Feltzen South and Blue Rocks, past the Ovens, on towards Cross Island.

We have a bit of wind — not enough to sail in, but enough to keep the sails asleep. A few young crew members make their way to the bow. Clustered behind the breast-hook or sitting on the bowsprit, they feel the ship rising up and tramping down into the rolling swell. For them, this is the beginning of a memorable summer, and they ask eagerly about the ship and her past.

Beyond the bowsprit lies an open, empty, pelagic horizon: a metaphor for the future, just as Lunenburg, now dimming behind the morning haze, is a metaphor for the past.

From my station in the bow, I look back at the schooner. This is the view I love best: the parallel lines of the deck planking, the buff dories stowed in the waterways under their royal blue covers, the gradual slope of the deck from the bowsprit down to the waist, the thicket of standing and running rigging beside each of the two masts, the long white curl of the rail cap, graceful as a fading note of music, sweeping down and inward on its way back to the quarterdeck a hundred and forty feet aft.

Today, on the first day of a new season, you might almost mistake her for a new ship — but her sparkling appearance is an illusion. She is in her twenty-ninth season, far past her normal life expectancy. She was built according to the Maritime tradition — and schooners constructed in that tradition were built quickly and cheaply, like bungalows in a subdivision, using unseasoned local wood — spruce, red oak, juniper, balsam fir. Their owners expected them to pay back their costs and turn a profit over a period of seven to ten years. If a wooden ship lasted more than a decade, the extra years were gravy. For all their heart-stopping beauty, the schooners were not built as works of art, designed for eternity; they were more like 18-wheelers, built to turn a profit by hauling freight or catching fish, and their projected life-spans were no longer than those of a semi-trailer.

Bluenose herself, a lucky ship, lived 25 years. At 29, *Bluenose II* is a glorious dowager with a splendid future behind her. She has endured this long only through a combination of good fortune, Lunenburg frugality and liberal applications of money.

Good fortune: white oak is the greatest boatbuilding wood found in temperate climates, and it lasts almost indefinitely. Warwick Tompkins' schooner *Wanderbird*, built of white oak, is still sailing after nearly a century. White oak is all but extinct in Europe, where it was used in the Viking longships and the wooden ships of England's sailing navy, the "hearts of oak" of early imperial Britain. It is not native to Nova Scotia, and it was not normally used in Maritime ships, but it is available in the southern United

States. When *Bluenose II* was built, Fred Rhuland had some
Carolina white oak on hand, left over from the construction
of *Bounty*. With it his shipwrights fashioned the backbone
— the keel and stem — of *Bluenose II*. And for her ceiling
— the inside planking of her hull — Rhuland used Douglas
fir, another prime northern wood.

That backbone has endured, while the other woods —
spruce, pine, birch, red oak — have been steadily rotting
away. Area after area has been replaced: miscellaneous
parts of the hull in the early 1970s, the timbers and planking in her bow and stern in 1976-77, an overall refit in
1982-83, the foremast in 1983-84, the bowsprit two years
later, the mainmast a year after that. In 1987-88 the transom
needed work; last winter the bow planking was stripped
away once more and the forward stanchions were re-
caulked. As Peter Brown says, the process is like painting
a bridge: as soon as you get to the end, you start all over
again.

The design itself also strains the hull. The keel is short,
about 50 feet long, only about one-third of her overall
length. The overhangs at bow and stern are enormous, and
their natural tendency is to droop. When this happens to a
ship, she is said to be "hogged": in effect her keel bellies
upward, the carefully-fitted planks twist away from one
another, the once-graceful curve of her rail straightens out,
and her future is short.

To prevent hogging, the shipyard places props the size
of telephone poles under *Bluenose II*'s bow as soon as she
is hauled out of the water, but her shape is distorted even
before the props go in place. Furniture which operates
properly when the ship is afloat suddenly rebels when she
is ashore. Doors won't close, drawers won't open. Slip her
back in the water, with her ends supported by their own
buoyancy, and everything works again.

That white-oak spine is the secret of the ship's long life,
and after nearly 30 years it still holds her together, soaked
with rot-arresting salt water, providing solid anchorage for
all the other parts of the ship. Still, despite all the precau-
tions, *Bluenose II* is distinctly hogged: six to eight inches out

of true in the 50-foot length of her keel. The backbone that has made it possible to go on repairing the ship all these years is finally giving up.

But it has not given up yet. On September 30, 1991, on her closing trip from Halifax to Lunenburg for layup, *Bluenose II* had a forecast of southwesterly winds of 15 to 20 knots, gusting to 25 — just right for a quick, relaxed trip. Instead, the wind drew into the west and rose to 40 knots. The schooner had her four lower sails set, and she roared off at 12 knots, rail down, covering fifty-odd sea miles in under five hours. By all accounts it was a thrilling ride.

Officials in the shipyard and the government were appalled. How could Barr have driven the aging ship so hard? What if she had popped a plank off and foundered? Maybe it was time for guidelines directing Barr not to sail her more than 25 miles offshore, not to carry much sail in strong winds, and so on.

To all such suggestions Don Barr responds with a polite snort.

"If she can't handle something like that, then she shouldn't be out there at all," he explains. "I don't know when I'm going to get caught in something like that — that breeze wasn't forecast, you know. Either she's safe to go to sea, or she's not safe to go to sea. But if she's going to go to sea, she has to take whatever the sea hands out, and you can't make guidelines for that."

In the spring of 1992, Scotia Trawler hauled her and pulled off a dozen planks all over the underbody, just to see what condition she was in. Some of those areas had not been examined since the ship was built in 1963. The structure was in amazingly good shape, and the Canadian Steamship Inspection service certified her for passenger service for another two years, until 1994. By then, however, major sections of the stern will have to be ripped open and rebuilt — and nobody can even estimate the costs; it is impossible to guess what kind of decay may be going on down there. But the price will probably be horrifying — and if the keel is gone, as it may well be, then *Bluenose II* will not be worth repairing. The price of replacing the backbone would go a long way towards replacing the entire ship.

Meet *Bluenose III.*

Bluenose III, as the proposed replacement schooner is now known, has been discussed on and off for a dozen years. As early as 1982, Tourism Minister Bruce Cochran noted that the province would soon have to make a major decision about replacing the schooner. A foundation was established, and successive tourism ministers have expressed their support for the project. In November 1991, then-Minister Terence Donahoe announced that the project would go ahead — and that the new ship would be built, like her predecessors, in Lunenburg.

Not everyone was charmed. Arthur F. Theriault is vice-president of A.F. Theriault and Sons, a well-regarded small shipyard in Meteghan River, Digby County. He wrote to the premier and the minister to express his "deep disappointment" that the province had already determined to give the contract to Lunenburg. *Bluenose III* would be an ambassador for the whole province; why shouldn't shipyards elsewhere have a chance to bid on the project?

The well-known columnist Harry Bruce was also opposed, though he raised a different objection. The original *Bluenose* had been "somewhat old-fashioned when it first hit the water in 1921," he noted; her mode of fishing was already being challenged by motor vessels. Her replica had cost the taxpayers millions of dollars. It made no sense to replicate her once again, when the same money could be put into "research into the science, design, navigation and construction of the great vessels of the future" or into "long-term promotion of the province's exports."

Perhaps — but Nova Scotia is only one of many small, poor states and provinces clamouring for the attention of the investors, tourists and traders, and *Bluenose II* carries the battle for publicity right into the chosen marketplace.

A week after she left Lunenburg, for instance, *Bluenose II* spent two days in Quebec City. Five hundred people per hour came aboard — nearly 9000 in two days — picking up French-language tourist literature and discovering that their language is alive and well in the Acadian communities of Nova Scotia. Every TV network in Quebec showed the ship's arrival. Radio Quebec did a 30-minute telecast about the ship, and Radio Canada did its weather forecasts from the deck in the middle of a "Canada 125" reception. The Quebec Museum of Civilizaton brought a crowd of 400 young people to tour the ship, and she was featured in colour on the front pages of Quebec's *Le Soleil* and the Montreal *Gazette*.

During an overnight stop in Trois Rivières 1500 visitors came aboard, and in Montreal the ship became a centrepiece in the celebrations surrounding the city's 350th anniversary. The Nova Scotia Department of Economic Development held a reception aboard for the Japan Trade Council, the Tourism Association of Nova Scotia staged an event for the travel industry, and Federal Transport Minister Jean Corbeil came aboard to kick off National Safe Boating Week.

And Quebec was not the main destination. The trip was conceived as a follow-up to the 1991 visit to Toronto when 30,000 people came aboard, along with 100 media representatives who showed her on programs ranging from Canada AM to MuchMusic.

"How do you otherwise buy that kind of coverage?" demands Peter Brown. "We've done commercial trade tours with the the provincial departments of fisheries, agriculture and culture as well as industry and tourism. In a city like New York, how do you attract industrial investors and tourism wholesalers to a seminar on your destination area without something to draw them — like a sail on *Bluenose II*? This whole trip to Ontario will cost about $70,000 to $80,000. I don't know any other way to get this kind of coverage for that kind of money."

Indeed, building a new vessel is itself not outrageously expensive. The new vessel herself will cost $5-6 million — enough to buy a handful of houses in Toronto or clean off the inventory of a good-sized car dealership. Another $2 million or so will be allocated to educational and promotional activities: creating a building site in Lunenburg that will allow visitors to watch the construction, and to document and explore the process in films, books, seminars, conferences.

Critics of the replacement schooner miss another salient point: the Province of Nova Scotia doesn't propose to pay for the new ship anyway. Like the RCMP Musical Ride, *Bluenose II* is one of Canada's very few unambiguous national symbols, known and loved across the country. Corporate Canada is well aware of her power as a symbol, and recognizes the commercial value of supporting her. As this is written, it appears that five major Canadian corporations will simply give the province the $8 million required to build and promote the new schooner. In return, they will be able to use the ship's image in their own advertising and promotion. After the vessel is launched, Nova Scotia will maintain and operate her.

The actual construction process creates another debate. Today's materials — fiberglass, steel, wood/epoxy, wood over metal frames — make it possible to build ships that will last indefinitely. Should *Bluenose III* be built in the traditional fashion, and replaced again in 20 or 25 years? Or is the spirit of *Bluenose* best expressed by some kind of innovation?

The debate goes on in public and in private, but the majority opinion is clear: a *Bluenose* built in some other medium is not a successor to *Bluenose*, but something else altogether. *Bluenose III* must be built by traditional methods. If the province chose another reasonably-similar method of construction — composite construction, for example, with wooden planks attached to metal frames — it would incur additional costs for research and development and re-training, and the eventual result would not really be an expression of the Lunenburg tradition.

"This type of vessel was built here by the hundreds," says Peter Brown. "The lines exist — the *vessel* exists, if you need to measure something — and the methods are well-known. It's no big deal. You don't need CAD-CAM work from the Technical University of Nova Scotia. We can just get on with it. The men in Lunenburg could start tomorrow."

But, say Brown and Barr, it would be a mistake to use the traditional local softwoods. This time, the schooner should be built of white oak, which is available and affordable, and though she will not last forever, she will last for a very long time. And she could be called *Bluenose II*, provided no other ship by that name is registered in Canada.

But *will* the schooner be the only ship of that name? In other words, what will happen to *Bluenose II*? Should she be kept afloat, perhaps as part of the Fisheries Museum of the Atlantic, like the *Theresa E. Connor*? Should she be sold — and if so, to whom and for what purpose? How much of her gear and equipment can be cannibalized and used in the new ship? Should she be hauled ashore and used as a spectacular "Welcome to Nova Scotia" sign beside the Trans Canada Highway at the New Brunswick border, as people in the border town of Amherst have suggested? Is there a way to make money with her? Could she be cut up and re-shaped into souvenirs?

To all such suggestions, Peter Brown simply shakes his head.

"Very painful to me and many others," he says. "But look: you don't want part of this ship turning up as a french-fry stand, and the cost of maintaining her at a museum would be worse than the costs we're facing now. Rot comes from fresh water; when you leave a wooden ship out in the rain, she rots from the top down. The *Theresa E. Connor* has cost more than $2.5 million over the last four years, just lying at the Fisheries Museum wharf. That's why the museum had to get rid of two of its ships; they couldn't afford to keep up with the rot." It's true: the museum finally gave up on *Reo II*, the once-powerful rum-runner, and *Cape North*, Nova Scotia's first dragger. They towed the two vessels out to sea and quietly sank them.

Could one make money with *Bluenose II* ? Not likely: the costs of maintenance would be huge, and they would steadily increase. No commercial venture yet suggested could absorb those costs and still turn a profit.

Souvenirs? The Boston National Historical Park at the Charlestown Navy Yard is right next to the USS *Constitution*, in the heart of the huge New England market. Souvenirs made of wood from the ship do not earn as much as $10,000 a year.

The consensus among those who know and love the ship is quite clear: remove any gear and equipment that is worth saving, and then give the beloved vessel a Viking funeral at sea. Tow her offshore, shed a tear, and sink her. Or, perhaps, sink her somewhere nearer to shore, possibly off the Ovens park in Lunenburg Bay. There, divers could visit her for a few years, until the waves and the teredoes reduce her timbers to silts and sediments, completing the eternal cycle of ships and the people who sail them. We come from the natural world, we dissolve back into it. *Requiescat in pace.*

Lulu and I join the officers for lunch in the saloon. Gigs has not lost his touch: the hearty beef stew, salad, and pie remind me that food is one factor which makes this a happy ship. We go back on deck to find the wind utterly vanished. *Bluenose II* slips along under diesel, her sails swaying idly as her hull rolls through the glossy round swells. We have passed the archipelago at the mouth of Mahone Bay, the Aspotogan Peninsula, the entrance to St. Margaret's Bay. Now the shaved grey rock of the shore is reaching out to us again from the early-summer haze.

"Sambro Light," says Don Barr, pointing to a red-and-white lighthouse alone on a bald rock. He points farther ahead, off the port bow. The swells are breaking over two massive ledges of rock, the water heaving up like the neck muscles of a Brahman bull, then charging in white fury across the stone. And this is almost a flat calm. We saw some nasty shoals in Lunenburg Bay this morning, but there is something chilling about these two ledges, like an exhalation of malign power.

"The Sisters," says Barr.

The Sisters! Phenomenal: I wrote a radio play based on a mordant folk tale about those rocks, but this is the first time I have actually seen them. One rock is called Blind

Sister: in the story, she was beautiful and beloved by a young fisherman, while her sighted sister was plain and destined for spinsterhood. Erupting in self-righteous jealousy, the sighted girl arranged for her blind sister to drown, and was herself drowned by their father. That is how the rocks got there, so they say.

They make me feel sick to my stomach.

Revise that. I am sick to my stomach. Oh, God. *Bluenose II* again. Am I going to disgrace myself before a new young crew by heaving the beef stew to the codfish and dolphins? Barr and I go on talking about the prospects and plans for the replacement schooner, but my attention is divided: I am listening carefully both to Barr and my belly, making contingency plans for a quick retreat to the heads, where perhaps I can unobtrusively be sick.

"Eight million dollars is not a lot of money as these projects go," Barr says, gazing at the passing shoreline. "When you talk about the Olympics, you're talking fifty, sixty, a hundred million. Eight million is a lot of money to you and me, though, that's the problem. People can grasp eight million." He's right: if the project required $80 million or $800 million, eyes would glaze over and minds would veer off elsewhere. But $8 million is an amount we could actually hope to command ourselves: people win more than that in government lotteries.

I am not going to be sick. A little breeze ruffles the water, and the ship's motion steadies. *Bluenose II* turns slowly to port, entering the approaches to Halifax Harbour. That huge 81-foot long boom swings far out to starboard as the wind comes aft. I chuckle to myself, remembering Peter Brown's experience trying to put up the ship's dress lights, all by himself, at Christmas.

The dress strings stretch from the bowsprit to the mastheads and then down to the tip of the boom. How do you get the string to the end of the boom, 17 feet out over the icy water of Lunenburg's harbour in December? Peter thought about that while he cleaned out all the sockets and tried all 193 bulbs — a dramatic experience, because he was plugging the strings in and out while reaming out the sockets with a screwdriver, and sometimes he confused the sequence and dug the screwdriver into a live socket. Flash! Snap!

He decided to lash seven broomhandles end to end, with a bent coat-hanger at the very tip. With this wobbly contrivance he proposed to poke a line through a shackle at the end of the boom, and then pull the lights out. It worked, eventually, but the first time he put the pole over the side it proved much heavier than he expected: it "swung down to the water in a beautiful arc and very nearly took me in too."

Brown was alone because the officers had all gone off to work on their own winter projects. They are on duty for 2000 hours during the season — a full year's work — so they take all their time off between October and April. Don Barr and his family have been using those long winter months to build a steel-hulled 65-foot Herreshoff schooner in Florida. His daughter did the welding, everyone pitched in on the painting and finish work. Barr shows photos of the spacious interior, gleaming with exotic varnished woods.

Now, after five winters, Barr's own schooner is almost ready for the water. When she is commissioned, the Barrs will sail for Panama and the Pacific, leaving her in Moorea, Suva, Bali or some other exotic place each summer while Barr transforms himself into the master of *Bluenose II* — or *Bluenose III*, as the case may be.

Delbé Comeau, meanwhile, is in the third year of building what he calls a "land ship" — a 2200-square-foot house in Meteghan River. The first winter he and a carpenter completed the foundation and the shell. He devoted the second winter to gyproc and paint, while tradesmen put in the plumbing and wiring. This fall he will install the cabinets and finish the trim. He and Mary expect to move in by Christmas.

Early in the afternoon, *Bluenose II* is motor-sailing at nine knots off Chebucto Head in bright sunlight with a warm south-westerly breeze. Don Barr gives a signal to Ron Ottens, and the engines subside into silence. *Bluenose II* scarcely falters: under sails alone, she continues at 8.5 knots, in sudden, shocking quiet. The flag snaps, the wake gurgles, and everyone suddenly smiles.

Once again I take the wheel as we enter a harbour. I had forgotten what a stinker she is to steer — heavy, slow reacting, unpredictable. She holds a steady course long enough to lull you, then suddenly veers off one way or the other. Marty Murrin is tolerant and quiet, but my steering is terrible, wavering back and forth in a ten-degree range. Still, it is the same remembered thrill: the big oaken spokes of the wheel in my hands, the deck sweeping forward, the spars and canvas wheeling against the blue summer sky.

Up ahead, a fleet of yachts is racing in the outer harbour. I turn over the wheel, and soon we are among them, waving and calling back and forth. Then we are slipping past Mauger's Beach, the long spit on McNab's Island immortalized by Thomas Raddall as "Hangman's Beach," where the British colonial and military regimes once erected gibbets on which to hang the tarred bodies of mutineers in chains, as a warning to rebellious sailors entering the port.

We sail for an hour, loping up the harbour past the harbour-mouth villages, the container terminal, the downtown waterfront condos. Below the office towers, off Historic Properties, Ron Ottens starts the engines again, idling into the wind while the crew lowers the sails and wrestles them into a tidy furl. The ship motors forward to her berth, looming bigger and bigger against the low stone buildings of the Halifax Sheraton and the restored waterfront. You can feel the excitement in the crew: for the new members, this is the very first arrival anywhere.

The great schooner slides into her home berth for the first time this season and stops as Ron Ottens puts the engines briefly into reverse. The wharf is choked with people in bright summer shorts, sun-hats and halters. Babies in strollers, white-haired couples, young families, people with cameras and video camcorders, filling the air with their voices and their cries. It feels like a holiday:

Canada Day, Labour Day, something like that. But it's only a lovely Saturday afternoon in May.

As soon as the gangplank is ashore, a sandy-haired man in sunglasses comes aboard.

"Good trip?" asks Peter Brown.

"Wonderful."

Peter glances over at the mob on the wharf.

"You know," he says, "there was hardly a soul around here until this ship came up the harbour, and then all of a sudden the place was packed. I don't know where they came from."

Bibliography

On Bluenose and Bluenose II:

Backman, Brian, and Backman, Phil. *Bluenose*. Toronto: McClelland and Stewart, 1965.

Bradley, Wendell P. *They Live by the Wind*. New York: Alfred A. Knopf, 1969.

Gillespie, G.J. *Bluenose Skipper: The Story of the Bluenose and Her Skipper*. Fredericton: Brunswick Press, 1955.

McLaren, R. Keith. *Bluenose and Bluenose II*. Willowdale Ont.: Hounslow Press, 1981.

Merkel, Andrew. *Schooner Bluenose*. Toronto: Ryerson Press, 1948.

Sultzbach, Michael C. *Canadian Schooner Bluenose*. M.Sc. thesis, Dalhousie University, 1978.

Ziner, Feenie. *Bluenose: Queen of the Grand Banks* (1970). Halifax: Nimbus Publishing, 1986.

Other related subjects:

Armour, Charles, and Lackey, Thomas. *Sailing Ships of the Maritimes*. Toronto: McGraw-Hill Ryerson, 1975.

Armstrong, Bruce. *Sable Island* (1981). Halifax: Formac, 1987.

Barss, Peter. *Images of Lunenburg County*. Toronto: McClelland and Stewart, 1978.

Chapelle, Howard. *The American Fishing Schooners, 1825-1935*. New York: W.W. Norton, 1973.

Church, Albert, and Connolly, James B. *American Fishermen*. New York: W.W. Norton, 1940.

Culler, R.D. *Skiffs and Schooners*. Camden, ME: International Marine Publishing, 1974.

Hayden, Sterling. *Wanderer*. New York: Alfred A. Knopf, 1963.

Horwood, Harold. *Bartlett: The Great Canadian Explorer*. Toronto: Doubleday, 1977.

Innis, Harold A. *The Cod Fisheries: The History of an International Economy*. Toronto: University of Toronto Press, 1940.

Kipling, Rudyard. *Captains Courageous* (1897). Toronto: Macmillan of Canada, 1964.

Maury, Richard. *The Saga of Cimba* (1939). Tuckahoe, N.Y.: John de Graff, 1971.

Mostert, Noel. *Supership*. New York: Alfred A. Knopf, 1974.

Pullen, H.F., and Jenson, L.B. *Atlantic Schooners*. Fredericton: Brunswick Press, 1967.

Thomas, Gordon. *Fast and Able: Life Stories of Great Gloucester Fishing Vessels*. Gloucester, MA: Gloucester 350th Anniversary Celebration, Inc., 1973.

Tompkins, Warwick. *Two Sailors*. New York: Viking Press, 1939.

Wallace, F.W. *Roving Fisherman*. Gardenvale, Que.: Canadian Fisherman, 1955.

About the Author

Silver Donald Cameron is one of Canada's most versatile authors. His recent best-seller, *Wind, Whales and Whisky: A Cape Breton Voyage* (1991) won the City of Dartmouth Book Award and the Atlantic Booksellers Choice Award. His other books include essays, social history, literary criticism, a thriller, *Dragon Lady*, and a young-adult novel, *The Baitchopper*.

More than fifty of Silver Donald Cameron's plays have been produced by CBC radio and he was recently a Gemini Award finalist for his half-hour TV drama *Peggy*, which also won several nominations and awards at film festivals. His short stories and articles have appeared in such magazines as *Saturday Night, Canadian Forum, The Nation* and *The Atlantic Monthly*. He has received National Magazine Awards for cultural reporting, travel writing, agricultural reporting, and service journalism.

Silver Donald Cameron and his wife, Lulu Terrio-Cameron, live with their son in a Halifax apartment, a renovated waterfront home in D'Escousse, Cape Breton, and aboard *Silversark*, a 27-foot cruising sailboat which they built themselves. He is currently writing a book about *Silversark's* recent voyage in the Gulf of St. Lawrence.